A World Out of Reach

A WORLD
OUT OF REACH

DISPATCHES FROM LIFE
UNDER LOCKDOWN

Selections from
The Yale Review's
"Pandemic Files"

Edited and with an Introduction by
MEGHAN O'ROURKE

Yale UNIVERSITY PRESS | NEW HAVEN & LONDON

IN ASSOCIATION WITH THE YALE REVIEW

Yale University Press books may be purchased in quantity for educational, business, or promotional use. For information, please e-mail sales.press@yale.edu (U.S. office) or sales@yaleup.co.uk (U.K. office).

Set in Gotham and Adobe Garamond types by Integrated Publishing Solutions, Grand Rapids, Michigan.
Printed in the United States of America.

Library of Congress Control Number: 2020942320
ISBN 978-0-300-25735-9 (paper: alk. paper)

A catalogue record for this book is available from the British Library.

This paper meets the requirements of ANSI/NISO Z39.48-1992 (Permanence of Paper).

10 9 8 7 6 5 4 3 2 1

To the memory of those who lost their lives to COVID-19
and
to the essential workers who kept the world running during the pandemic

Contents

CONTENTS

APRIL

MAY

CONTENTS

JUNE

CONTENTS

Introduction

In January I started reading obsessively about the novel coronavirus that was racing through Wuhan, China. I was finishing writing a book about contested chronic illnesses and the role viruses play in them, and I have an amateur's interest in disease, especially poorly understood ones. A friend of mine, a longtime science reporter, had drilled into me that the world was overdue for a pandemic, and I wondered if this was it. Each night as I read, the developing story seemed startlingly different from the one I'd read the night before. First the story was an account of a new virus affecting a handful of people at a wet market in Wuhan—a story about animal to human transmission, in other words, and perhaps about the dangers of wet markets and climate change driving us to eat a wider range of animals, exposing ourselves to dangerous new viruses. The next day there was a story about how many people in the city had this virus, which was alarming, because it suggested a gap between what we thought we knew about the virus and what we actually knew about it. This virus had to be transmitting from person to person. Days later, there it was in the newspaper: a story about evidence of human to human transmission of the novel coronavirus, now known as SARS-CoV-2.

As the days passed and the news worsened, I felt dread rise in me. Even as I sat in my children's dim room, warmed by the glow of the nightlight, watching my boys—well fed, clean, and cozy in their pajamas, as safe and well as I could ever make them—play with their blocks, I knew a pandemic was coming. Over the next weeks, before cases were known to be in the United States, I canceled travel and prepared for the worst, following the instructions of a virologist friend who told me to buy extra supplies at the store each time I went shopping. Even so, it was still a shock in March when, seemingly in one stroke, Connecticut (where I live), New York, and New Jersey shut down. One day I was at a friend's book party, shouting over the house music and sharing tapas; the next our son's preschool was closing, and a curfew and then a lockdown were imposed on the state.

Overnight the world was lost to us. I vividly remember, as many of us must, those first days of sitting inside, looking out the window at the still-bare branches of the March trees, then seeing the first buds of green, and knowing that time was passing. Inside, our days were a parade of small tasks: getting the children fed, dressed, entertained, set up for preschool with Zoom; trying, somehow, to put in a workday; then doing everything in a kind of reverse—undressing the children, bathing them, getting them to bed. Time scalloped, looping in on itself. At one point, on the night of the supermoon, an ambulance and a fire truck came down our street. We watched as the EMTs and firemen painstakingly put on their PPE (personal protection equipment) before going in to our neighbor's house and bringing him out on a stretcher. My sons, aged three and eighteen months, were delighted to have the close-up view of the flashing lights. "Weee-ooo!" said the baby, pointing at the ambulance. He was ecstatic; I was chilled.

WHO ARE WE—who were we—in the pandemic? As some answers grow clearer with time, others become dimmer. Collected in this book are attempts to answer this question. The emergence of the novel coronavirus has disrupted nearly every aspect of our lives and transformed American life in ways we can't fully understand yet. We will need historians and political scientists and novelists to wrap their minds around the full scope—the ramifications—of this pandemic; the future will be able to see things that we can't yet process. It will know the depth of the virus's economic fallout; it will know when the vaccine arrived, if one did; it will know if a treatment was developed, or if and how the virus mutated, becoming less or more dangerous to human health. It will take stock of the ways we have failed one another—the mass graves at Hart Island, explored by Kathryn Lofton in the pages that follow; the structural implications of pandemics, investigated by Octávio Ferraz; the shameful treatment of the vulnerable populations of incarcerated citizens at Rikers Island and other jails, as Russell Morse captures. Yet the future will also assess the ways Americans rose up to demand change, especially in the Black Lives Matter protests of late May and June, chronicled here to great effect by Hafizah Geter and Roger Reeves.

But what the future won't know, exactly, is what it felt like in the moment. How in the first months, each week felt like a distinct new chapter of experience; how rapidly the virus seemed to spread in the Northeast, and with it misinformation; how it felt to watch President Trump's afternoon task force meetings, with their bizarre and performative scripts, knowing that they were part propaganda while also clinging to the shreds of information to be found within them. The future won't remember what it felt like when our children, our parents, our partners began coughing, running a fever, feeling unwell, and how desperately powerless we felt, how hard it was to get masks, tests, gloves, in those first weeks (it is hard to remember even now). The future can't experience how life seemed to go from normal to frozen almost overnight, so that for a few days it almost felt as if we were just on spring break (and many of us were—the lockdown started over the break at Yale University, where *The Yale Review* is housed), until the sirens started splitting the silence of the night. Only we who lived through it can know how steep the learning curve was for all of us, from doctors and other health care workers to civilians, or how the pressures of lockdown led to social upheaval.

That's where the idea for the "Pandemic Files" emerged, out of the desire to have writers reflect on their lived response to the unfolding global crisis, almost as it happened. These responses were published as an ongoing collection on our website as the pandemic unfolded. Taken together, they aim to capture life in the age of the novel coronavirus, with dispatches, think pieces, meditations, poems, and essays on key aspects of the epidemic. In the pages that follow, we present a selection of those works, arranged mostly in the order in which they were written, works that try to answer the question of who we were during the pandemic. Within you will find short essays on history and medicine; reported features on the intersection of the pandemic with issues such as work on Trump's border wall in Arizona; poems; and—to open the book—an eerie short story by the brilliant novelist Katie Kitamura that plays with looking both forward and backward in time to capture the feeling we all had of wondering who would prove to be right, and about what, back before the pandemic arrived. And you will, of course, find elegies: for people lost (Rachel Jamison Webster's beautiful essay in tribute to her aunt Cynthia, Rowan Ricardo Phillips's poem for his grandmother, and Emily Greenwood's meditation on Thucydides, her father, and George Floyd), as well as for a world that is gone. The contributors come from around the world, just as the *Review*'s contributors always do, but we made a point of seeking work from a number of Yale students and faculty to register the pandemic's local impacts as well as its global ones.

In other words, this is a compendium more than a sleekly focused anthology constellating around a single question or mode. For the editors of the *Review,* this pluralism of response is the very point: We wanted to hear from a diversity of minds in motion over the questions troubling them in the first months of the pandemic. Of course, because this is a selection from a specific moment in time, there are many subjects not included here that feel urgent to us, too: what it was like to be a senior citizen in this moment; what it was like to survive a bad case of the virus or to become one of the "long haulers," those for whom the virus didn't resolve tidily; the crisis in child care for parents with young children; and what the long-term economic effects of the pandemic will be, to name just a few. But it is our hope that these pieces might help encapsulate both the inexpressible grief of our moment and the possibility for change and reflection held within it, offering a sense of the pandemic as its reality was being felt, thought through, and metabolized by the nation.

We chose the title *A World Out of Reach* for its multiple meanings: it speaks not only to how many of us felt during lockdown—our former world now out of reach beyond our windowpanes—but also to the ways in which the failings of this moment intensified a yearning for a better world beyond our grasp.

What we don't know yet is how death on this scale will change us, or even if it will. The world continues; the virus is still out there as I write. By the time you read this, the world will be different many times over. We will know more about the various waves of the virus; perhaps—one can hope—we will have made some changes happen. Having lost the world, we might be able, suddenly, to see it anew. What is out of reach may, if we desire it enough, inspire us again to reach.

Meghan O'Rourke
June 22, 2020

A World Out of Reach

Do You Know Alex Oreille

Katie Kitamura

Despite the imminent outbreak in our city, we had taken ourselves to a reading at a small bookshop by the waterfront. There were more people than we thought there would be, and although by that point we had already been told not to shake hands, although we had been inundated with warnings not to touch our faces, people were embracing as though we were not on the verge of catastrophe.

About the reading itself I remember very little. In normal times I would have enjoyed it, but these were not normal times. I was distracted. It had been weeks since I had slept well. At night I was plagued by dreams of contamination. By day I tracked the progress of the virus, noting as it slowly, and then suddenly, made its way to our city. Now the first case had arrived, and we had been told there were likely hundreds more, still undiagnosed.

After the reading, my husband and I stood around and made unfunny jokes about the coming pandemic, but mostly we refused to touch other people. I don't remember when I first noticed the young woman. She had a very plain face—even now I would struggle to describe it in concrete terms. Mousy brown hair, medium height, quite large and expressive eyes.

She had been standing a few feet away for some time, examining the bookshelves, before she suddenly introduced herself. "Excuse me," she said. "But do you know Alex Oreille? I overheard you say that you were at Covington in October. He was there at the same time."

I turned to the young woman as she continued.

"Red hair? Tall? Funny walk?"

The name was unfamiliar, and I had no immediate recollection of the person she described. But as she pantomimed the comic gait and manner of her friend, an image of a young man began to form in my mind, the hazy recollection of someone who might have been Alex Oreille.

"I'm not sure," I said sincerely. "But yes, probably. The name is familiar. Did he like Covington?"

She nodded. "Oh yes," she said. Her face and limbs were marvelously mobile; as she spoke she flung her arms and hands about, occupying the air around us. "He finished his manuscript, he made a bunch of friends, he lived in a beautiful place by the sea." Lowering her voice, she continued, "To be honest, it's hard not to be jealous. I'm working on the HIV vaccine. Sometimes it seems like there's only ever one update: 'It didn't work.'" She screwed up her face and gave a clownish shrug and my husband and I laughed. She laughed too, quite loudly.

My husband said, "So you study infectious disease? Can you talk to us about the virus?"

"I can talk, for sure," she said slowly. She raised a theatrical eyebrow. "But I don't want to bore you—"

"You won't bore us," he said. "Trust me."

She clasped her hands and began. "For the vast majority of people, it's nothing more than a cold. A headache, a sore throat—a bad flu at most. But for a percentage of people it's much worse. It degrades into pneumonia. It results in hospitalization, and in some cases death."

She paused. "If you look at all the statistics coming out of China, not one child has been seriously ill. It's the elderly and the immuno-compromised. People with underlying conditions—which is a sub-stantial number of people in many parts of the United States."

As she spoke, I felt a slow creep of impatience. She hadn't told me anything I didn't already know, nothing that couldn't be found in the course of a casual internet search, the kind I had been performing for days. As she began to rattle off statistics that could be found on the website of a well-known university, my husband shifted his weight on his feet.

She looked around the room and lowered her voice confiden-tially. "I would say right now in this room, three or four people are infected."

I looked up, startled. "Here? Right now? But there are only twenty of us."

As if of its own volition, my husband's hand crept into his pocket and withdrew a small bottle of hand sanitizer.

She smiled and leaned forward, so that her face was mere inches from ours. "Exactly. The virus is everywhere. It's too late."

We left the bookshop shortly after that. It was too unnerving to be in that room of people. We said our good-byes and then pulled on our coats and scarves and made our way downstairs. As I pushed the door open—touching the metal handle with my bare hand before brushing the hair out of my face, something that would soon become inconceivable—I turned and saw the young woman again.

She was on the other side of the room, talking animatedly with a young man who worked in the bookshop, her big and buoyant ges-tures legible from across the room.

"I can talk, for sure," I heard her say. "But I don't want to bore you—"

We stepped out into the cold air. My husband asked if I wanted to take the subway or order a car. I turned and looked back through the plate-glass windows of the bookshop. I couldn't hear what the woman was saying but I saw the young man recoil. No doubt she was telling him that right now in that room, there were three or four people who were infected . . .

We took the subway home. Those were the last cold days before the weather began to warm. As we stood in the crowded car, I said that I had a terrible headache. My husband told me his throat was throbbing, and then we stared at each other in silence. By the next day, the number of cases in the city had tripled. By the following week, the city would be placed under a lockdown order.

Later, many months—or perhaps it was years—later, after the lockdowns and the protests, after the pandemic had passed and a vaccine found—we would come across people in the newly awakened city. People who, in the days before the outbreak, had also met a young woman with expressive features, an infectious-disease specialist with a friend called Alex Oreille.

It had happened in bars, at gigs, at dinner parties and birthday gatherings. They all remembered her and her peculiarly named friend. The specific details of her biography were disputed—it had been the research hospital downtown rather than uptown, she had said Ebola, not HIV, she had been visiting from Seattle, or possibly San Francisco or Chicago. But we all remembered the same lines, spoken with such panache. *The virus is everywhere. It's too late. I don't want to bore you—*

I recalled her youth, her unprepossessing manner, the fact that she had told me nothing other than what I already knew. Had there been a certain relish to the way she had shared her calamitous prediction? Hadn't she been too cheerful a Cassandra? But in those days, we were ravenous for information, and all too credulous. What we craved in those long weeks and months and years, what we were searching for, was certainty.

After the final lockdown was lifted, we stepped out of our homes. We looked at the new leaves on the trees, the iron posts on the gate, the sunlight falling on all of it. We looked with such hunger that each detail was near blinding. It was not the same world as before.

MARCH

Cannon Fodder

Laura Kolbe

War and Peace is making a comeback this spring, along with other great fat books, book clubbing in general, twelve-bean soups, and other projects meant to reacquaint us with a more glacial, less contemporary sense of time. When I think of *War and Peace* now, though, my mind strays from the Rostovs and Bezukhovs to Charles Joseph Minard's graphs of Napoleon's invasion of Russia. Minard was a nineteenth-century French civil engineer esteemed for his data-rich but immediately apprehensible diagrams of everything from commuter traffic to wine imports. His most famous and damning image, however, maps the progress of the Napoleonic army as it staggered west from Russia back to central Europe. Soldiers' lives are initially a thick red band, a gash of enormous and emphatic force. Each millimeter of red width stands for ten thousand men. As the march continues, the red band dwindles, etiolates. By the end of the campaign only a small stream trickles back to safely held territory.

As a child, I went to a somewhat old-fashioned Catholic school where history was largely understood as the study of military battles and their outcomes. This kind of education leaves much out, but it does help me recognize a Minardian or Napoleonic situation when I see one. It's becoming rapidly apparent that I, an internal-medicine doctor based at two academic hospitals in Manhattan, am part of the thick red band that's about to be wrung threadbare.

In the Trump administration's United States, COVID-19 has always been about commodities—that is, their scarcity. First there weren't enough tests, and the available tests were sporadically employed and sluggish to yield results. Then there were too many probable cases for it to be practicable to test widely, and besides, we somehow ran out of the swabs needed for the test assays (just as there were finally almost enough of the latter). I'm speaking in the national "we," and in particular the New York "we." Here in New York City we've mostly stopped testing all but the severely ill who are sick enough to need a hospital bed—it would be a waste of precious swabs. While we worried about tests and swabs, we ran out of personal protective equipment for health care workers.

Over the course of two weeks my hospital's stock of gowns, gloves, masks, and face shields visibly dwindled in every cabinet. Eventually you had to know whom to ask about secret cabinets, small locked stashes. It helped to whisper; it helped to have friends. My head was full of combination codes for various locked drawers and closets around the hospital. Then even the locked chambers started to empty. Now, every day we are told that a modest quantity of new supplies are almost here, but every day they're not quite here. Ditto for ventilators. There is a growing array of formal and informal protocols for cleaning, reusing, stretching, and sharing everything from masks to rooms to ventilators, all ingenious but admittedly not quite as good as the gold standards for worker safety or patient care. This is ubiquitous in all the hospitals in our region, with mine, in fact, faring better than most. In addition to finding or reusing scarce equipment, new aspects of my job include lengthy and heartbreaking conversations about prognosis and "code status" (a patient's wish for resuscitation and/or a ventilator), determining which patients' deaths are imminent enough that they can be allotted their single hour-long visit from the loved one of their choice (otherwise, no visitors allowed), and studying textbooks and videos so that I might serve as an ICU critical care doctor should the need arise (which normally would require an extra two years of intensive training beyond the medical education I've had). Each day some of the patients on my list are critically ill, and some are recovering. I quiz those who are recovering more extensively about their living conditions than I ever would have before. A single male taxi driver living with six other men in a studio in Queens, where they sleep in shifts on a row of cots? Not safe for him to go home, even though his personal prognosis is good and we desperately need his hospital bed for new arrivals.

What feels distinctly different this week is that as more volunteers begin reporting for training and deployment—early-graduated medical students and retired, part-time, or private-practice clinicians, some to do direct clinical work, others to offload phone calls and other aspects of social work and public health—the governmental and corporate-sector response seems palpably less worried about the situation on the ground. If you have enough infantry, you can countenance a good deal of loss. Operations can continue even if many are out sick.

It seems to me that much of this scarcity could have been mitigated if the inventory of all public- and private-sector PPE and ventilators had immediately been requisitioned by a federal public health force, to be deployed as needed to areas of crisis around the country. Instead, individual hospitals, cities, and states all remain in protracted and mutually destructive bidding wars that delay even basic protections for hospitals approaching or experiencing crisis. This week, for example, the proposed collaboration between GM and Ventec to make ventilators appears to be stalling because the parties cannot agree on a price. Today, somehow, our hospital's uptown campus got a hundred more ventilators. This is fantastic (though belated, and not nearly as many as we need); at the same time, I know that this same day, downtown and across the river are people for whom ventilators are indicated but who are going without, and who will die. Almost certainly, people I glimpsed at work today were exposed to the virus, and will sicken next week.

If I haven't already, I will almost certainly either contract COVID-19 or become an asymptomatic carrier of disease to others. Despite my best efforts, I touch and approach too many people and things—carefully and hygienically, but not infallibly. The odds are overwhelmingly in my favor to have a mild case at most. But aggregated across the city and the region, large numbers of health care workers will be severely ill next week because of shortages and shortcuts last week, and so on and so forth, perhaps into summer.

Despite all this, somehow morale is high where I work. I am overtaken by giddy surges of love and commitment and awe as I gaze around our offices and wards at the nurses, physician assistants, doctors, respiratory therapists, custodians, techs, and transport workers—my fellow infantry. I'm learning names, ashamed that it took me this long. Other colleagues confess to feeling the same, despite years of building sturdy dams separating work from emotion. Of course, the paradox of my growing scope of love and concern—the rising number of people whom I now care about deeply and individually—is that it raises my odds of experiencing a direct blow of grief and mourning.

In the meantime, some of us look forward to reusing the oddball array of helpful and unhelpful-but-striking garments and headgear sent to us by generous and well-intentioned tailors and construction workers and others, whenever it next becomes feasible to protest the political situation in the streets. Let our weird apparel remain a symbol of "making do" when we should never have had to. For now we are very much at work.

There's a Sickness Outside

Nitin Ahuja

Soon I'll start another weeklong rotation as the rounding gastro-enterologist at my hospital, where, as expected, cases of COVID-19 are on the rise. Lately my nonmedical friends have been offering up their spontaneous thanks for the work I do, which flatters me, and makes me a little sad, and heightens my sense that I'm walking into a different world—a world of risk. This week, with my usual office hours on hold, I've mostly been at home, texting colleagues, reading headlines, and taking account of what gives me comfort and what gives me pause. I derive comfort, for instance, from the idea of ventilators as closed circuits, the infected lungs of a mechanically supported patient sealed off by plastic tubes from the rest of the world. I'm given pause when I remember that the coronavirus is transmitted in so many ways, including through the feces that I regularly encounter in procedural settings. Comfort: thermal checks at hospital entrances, and a policy that no employee with a fever will be allowed in. Pause: rapidly depleting stores of respiratory masks, normally discarded and replaced with every encounter, now limited to one per provider every few days.

Sometimes I imagine throwing that mask aside and striding youthfully, heroically, into the fray—entering patients' rooms as before, in my starchy white coat, sorting out the story of their bowel habits, placing my stethoscope ceremonially upon their rumbling abdomens and crackling chests. Against their labored breathing I'd keep mine measured, resigned to illness, the odds decent enough that I'll eventually recover. But there's no real claim to martyrdom in a pandemic, when every victim becomes a vector. So my attention returns to these symbols of leakiness and enclosure, these energized borders at various scales—the sliding glass doors of the intensive care unit, the rooftop helipad and ambulance bay, the bare skin intermittently exposed between my gown and gloves.

PROFESSIONAL DIALOGUE surrounding COVID-19 follows the basic precepts of germ theory, the late-nineteenth-century discovery that a specific pathogen will trigger a specific cascade of physiologic dysfunction. Predictably, microbiology research efforts have focused on reliable testing and treatment for those germs, efforts that rely upon and reinforce a particular understanding of our physical selves: that we are each a closed system facing discrete and measurable external threats, which enter our bodies in defined ways—in the case of respiratory infections, for example, most often via the mouth and nose. Confronted with the challenge of this new pandemic, however, such confidence easily falls away. Instead we fall into older patterns of thinking about illness, in which threat seems to come at us from all sides, in which our physical selves feel dangerously porous to the strange, potent world we inhabit.

This thinking dates back to antiquity and is built on a sense of the body's inherent and continuous vulnerability to infiltration. In *Inescapable Ecologies,* the historian Linda Nash refers to these two models as the "modern body" and the "ecological body." The modern body is the body of the early twentieth century, ascending in parallel with the medical laboratory, where fluid analyses and imaging techniques promote the ideal of complete internal legibility. It is a mechanical body, divided rationally into systems that can be subdivided into component parts, each of which might be studied for isolated pathology. The ecological body, by contrast, is unpredictable and irreducible. It reflects properties of humoral balance, the ancient concept of vital fluids dictating one's personal temperament, and of environmental balance, health supported or disrupted by subtle changes in weather and landscape. The key distinction between these models is the question of permeability, which is insignificant to the modern body but foundational to the ecological one. Prior pandemics, from malaria to the Black Death, were explained by the concept of miasma—noxious vapors emanating from some hidden source, sickening whoever had the bad luck of passing through them.

Our early response to the coronavirus pandemic borrows from both ideas of the body. The ubiquitous images in popular media of the SARS-CoV-2 particle—a gray sphere studded with thorny red projections—aim to identify the threat and make it visible, inviting us to remember its basic materiality. And yet we grapple constantly with the pathogen's elusiveness. These days, to walk into an emergency department or through a drugstore or along a narrow city street is to reckon with a sense of dread at the prospect of those barbed particles suspended in the air or coating the countertops and shelves. It is an old-fashioned dread, miasmatic—the sort we might presume germ theory to have cleanly displaced.

If laboratory methods gave us our modern bodies, the protracted lack of those methods during the COVID-19 crisis has made space again for turning back toward premodern sensibilities. Were hospitals and communities suddenly flooded with an infinite supply of rapid viral swabs, or if a reliable antibody screen were developed or a vaccine approved for use tomorrow, we would watch the apprehension receding in real time. Clear lines could be drawn around sick individuals, in turn legitimizing an approach to this sickness as a single disease entity; we could begin to separate the susceptible from the immune. But for now we are forced to scrutinize whatever data we can find to organize this affliction and its various potential courses, from pulmonary to hematologic to gastrointestinal, from mild to moderate to severe.

So far, these data have left ample space for ambiguity. We note differences from one country's data to the next; certain families appear inordinately devastated while others are spared. What looks like an interplay between virus and personal constitution unravels one disease into many. Each harrowing story of a young, otherwise healthy adult who dies from complicated pneumonia raises the question of what went wrong. Was there an inborn vulnerability that might otherwise have stayed hidden, some deep-seated loophole for the virus to exploit? Against the grain of age-related mortality curves runs the still scarier notion that when faced with exposure, some of us might be preconfigured for doom.

THE ANXIETY induced by the pandemic's hazy boundaries corresponds to an urgency to shore up life's more recognizable borders. We retreat into our homes, the rooms and corners we know best, and encourage our loved ones to do the same. We take a head count, stock the pantry, and lock the door. Social distancing makes sense on a public health basis—but also on a visceral one. Leaving for work from my apartment building in Philadelphia, I feel a rush of relief upon finding the maintenance man spraying disinfectant on all the elevator buttons. To explain to my Hindi-speaking grandmother why her nursing home no longer welcomes visitors, my father keeps it simple: *bimari hai bahr*—there's a sickness outside. For a few of my friends, the headache of canceled international travel has rapidly given way to the mere nuisance of shipping delays on their hand soap orders.

Several of the bodies we worry over are concentric, and it is hard to hold them all in mind at once. Nested within the country are states, municipalities, and families, with risk pushing some at every level into a defensive posture. On the internet I, like many, have seen the video of two women fighting over six rolls of toilet paper, scrolled past pictures of a California gun shop with a line stretching around the block. A few days ago our hospital leadership began asking employees via email to give back any protective equipment they might have stowed away in their private possession. As the crisis lingers and sickness closes in, many people are drawing progressively tighter perimeters.

I have fears about how the situation could deteriorate, the worst of which impel me toward the superstitious belief that it is somehow safer to leave them unspoken. What I can say is that I'm afraid this sickness will remain indistinct and pervasive for months, leading to consequences I'd taken for granted were out of bounds, like life support for the oldest or sickest patients being prescriptively withdrawn, or stones being thrown through neighborhood store windows. Presumably either of these eventualities—the foundering of social or ethical norms—could further erode the motivation of health care workers to keep working. I'm likewise afraid of the collapse of my own hospital's departmental divisions, leading to a makeshift critical-care unit being staffed by whoever is available to serve. As has happened in Italy, I might no longer be a gastroenterologist, or perhaps even much of a doctor, really, as much as a set of (hopefully) useful hands.

With these forecasts in mind, I've been recalling what I once knew about acute respiratory distress syndrome (ARDS), the life-threatening condition associated with the most severe cases of COVID-19. In it, the virus triggers a robust inflammatory reaction that weakens the lungs' capillary walls, causing fluid to leak into the millions of microscopic sacs called alveoli where oxygen and carbon dioxide are normally exchanged. Patients with ARDS are usually placed on ventilators—now in short supply—that force oxygen past the fluid filling the lungs and into the circulating blood. In patients infected with coronavirus, the need for a ventilator might last for weeks, each mechanical breath trying to keep all those tiny compartments functional and intact, pushing back against the inflammatory tide.

Health care providers, as distinct from public health professionals, are trained to focus on individual patients, looking after one at a time. It's rare that we have to consider the simultaneous dissolution of other systems, whether supply chains, the social fabric, or our own bodies. Deficiencies in diagnostic certainty and infrastructural support have fostered another kind of leakiness at the bedside, an intensification of medicine's empathetic foundations—the hunch that soon we too will be lying flat on our backs with tubes down our throats. As the air all around us goes foul, which borders matter most? Like many in my field, I'm fortifying barriers between myself and everyone I love, knowing that those barriers might stay up forever, imposing a vast emotional toll, including the horror of dying alone. Unconstrained, this virus keeps flickering into fog; every day more people get lost in it. How best to hold the line? Is there a line at all?

Medicine's Innovation Problem

Rena Xu

The tongue-in-cheek observation of "tradition unimpeded by progress" has always seemed to contain a kernel of truth when applied to health care. Historically, change has not been our medical system's strong suit. But as COVID-19 sweeps across the nation, wreaking havoc on society and placing unprecedented strain on health care infrastructure, the need for system-wide innovation becomes more critical than ever.

Innovation doesn't just refer to the race to develop a vaccine, or even the scramble to rig ventilators for multi-patient use, repurpose ships into hospitals, or fashion protective masks out of home supplies, as important as these extraordinary efforts may be. It also applies to more ordinary challenges—challenges that many hospitals were ill prepared to face even before the current crisis. In overbooked clinics, wait times are long and visits are short. Patients spend hours on the phone trying to get their symptoms triaged, their questions answered, their prescriptions refilled. Frequently they get routed to the wrong specialists; after waiting weeks or months for an appointment, they learn that they really needed to see someone else. In other instances, not knowing where to turn, they seek care in the wrong places—going to the emergency department for nonurgent issues, for instance, or trying to self-diagnose from online information.

While these challenges predated the pandemic, they will be far more pronounced in a post-COVID world. Many hospitals, quite sensibly, are canceling nonessential doctors' visits and procedures to preserve precious capacity. But disease processes don't halt in a pandemic, and patients with medical issues other than COVID-19—cancer, chronic illness, even so-called elective needs—require attention, too. Our medical system is not prepared to handle this backlog. Put another way: if we are lucky enough to flatten the curve, the next great challenge will be managing the long tail—not just of COVID patients but of countless others. Doing so successfully will be possible only if we are willing to embrace creative measures, and quickly.

Hospitals and medical practices have been particularly slow to change when it comes to matters of workflow. Capabilities that are commonplace in our day-to-day lives—conducting business virtually, for instance, or making and managing appointments online—are still used tentatively, or not at all, in medicine. Telemedicine offers an informative case study. While the technology itself has been around for decades, use of it is nowhere near mainstream, at least until recent weeks. Now, adoption of telemedicine is skyrocketing and garnering significant attention. Connecting virtually with a doctor, we're learning in quarantine, can be as easy as FaceTiming with family or conducting a business meeting over Zoom. Though far from perfect, such technologies offer opportunities for connecting those who are otherwise kept apart.

This breakthrough is due not only to the novel coronavirus but also to two important changes made in response to it. The first is in insurance coverage. Previously, under Medicare, only patients in rural areas were eligible for telemedicine coverage, and only if they traveled to designated medical facilities to access the service. Now the Center for Medicare and Medicaid Services (CMS) has temporarily modified its regulations to reimburse for telemedicine services regardless of where patients are located. An increasing number of states have mandated that private payers reimburse telemedicine services at the same rates they would offer for in-person services—so-called payment parity—and some insurers have expanded telemedicine coverage for their members.

The second change is in physician licensure. As part of their emergency response to the pandemic, the federal government and several states have relaxed restrictions on providers' ability to practice across state lines. Historically, this has been a major barrier to the adoption of telemedicine. Getting licensed in a single state is hassle enough—start to finish, it took me five months to get licensed as a urologic surgeon in Massachusetts—and requiring separate medical licenses for each state, many doctors long have argued, is as unnecessary as requiring separate drivers' licenses to cross state borders.

These regulatory modifications are timely, but also belated. It shouldn't take a pandemic to convince the medical system to support the use of a telephone. Like many, I wonder whether the progress made now will be sustained after the crisis ends—whether this brief experiment in virtual care, much like a free trial, will be enough to catalyze permanent change.

But beyond that, I wonder what other barriers to innovation, regulatory or otherwise, are still in place and don't need to be. The fact that we are collectively navigating uncharted territory right now presents a unique opportunity to jump-start other measures that, like the adoption of telemedicine, should have happened long ago.

Opportunities for change abound at virtually every step of the care continuum. We need smarter ways to triage patients—to get them the right evaluations in the right settings in the right time frame. We need more efficient and responsive mechanisms for pairing care supply and demand so that patients see the appropriate doctors based on their specific medical needs, and providers' schedules are neither overbooked nor underfilled. We need to divide and conquer medical visits, potentially leveraging virtual pre-visits with nonphysician staff to help focus patients' discussions with their doctors. And we need to scale back bureaucratic tasks so that clinicians can dedicate their time and energy to saving lives. The list goes on.

Many private enterprises have already developed solutions to address these very issues, from Zocdoc's online appointment scheduling to Kyruus's algorithmic patient-provider matching. Numerous start-ups have built tools for symptom triaging, patient education, and care navigation. But health systems themselves have yet to adopt such changes on a meaningful scale. None of these innovations entails particularly groundbreaking technology, but they all require considerable resources and willingness on the part of many—clinicians and administrators alike—to learn new ways of working.

While health care workers will play an essential part in executing these changes, they cannot do so without the right regulatory environment and the right leadership from the institutions where they work. This is a pivotal moment in which we need health systems to embrace innovative solutions, policy makers to provide funding and regulatory support, and insurers to allow for progressive reimbursement structures. Before last month, many in the medical field perceived a stark choice: between practicing within the status quo and seeking progress outside of clinical practice. Now, suddenly, that dichotomy seems outdated. It's time to demand a third option and bring innovation into the core of our medical system, where it is needed most.

March 11

Alicia Mireles Christoff

The U.S. is getting serious about social distancing and I am trying to
have a baby

Love in the time of: the T is empty-ish and the clinic is full
All the numbers are bad: 9% conception rate Clomid + IUI, 21% IVF
5.7% COVID-19 mortality rate, according to WHO

I wait to have blood drawn: 9 vials, 2 lab techs, gossiping brightly
about a third co-worker they can't stand

In the lobby I read "March 3" by Eileen Myles: a poem creates a soft
hole in the day

Down the street from the hospital I order *pupusas* and hate my 3rd-
gen "thank you"
I listen to the easy roll of Español that fills the room and feel a pelagic
sadness

I wander Longwood and FaceTime my friends crying from the concrete plaza outside Stop & Shop
Motherhood is lonely decisions, they say
I mouth a distracted "I'm sorry" to a man who shuffles by asking for
change and notice his face chapped white at the line where lip becomes skin

Yesterday the governor declared a state of emergency and I am the capitol reacting

The day soft holes into NY 9/11 when downtown was closed and I couldn't go back to my dorm: I walked to Old Navy to buy a sweat-shirt and sat on a bench in the mid-30s clutching the logoed plastic bag I'd filled with my Norton anthologies
Soft holes into March 2000 when my dad dropped dead of a heart attack and my sisters and I drove to the mall to buy new clothes for the funeral

It's warm this week, unseasonable, and snowdrops are pushing through the soil on the Common
The first spring flowers, they bow their crowns to winter

Across the state my students have their own evacuation orders
They worry the cost of plane tickets, of home
The seniors go out drinking and drop tears on each other

In DC they are pushing through a coronavirus bill with holes in it

38 y/o females make eggs without qualities
In her office the doctor had drawn circles with columns of Xs lined up inside to show how cells split without dividing genetic material evenly

Near the state house a woman misses a step coming out of the liquor store and falls down on the sidewalk
She gets up slowly and I watch my own pitiful calculations: does she need help, can I touch her

The Lice

Miranda Featherstone

One morning the week that cases of COVID-19 began to multiply in earnest across the East Coast of the United States, I found a louse in my daughter's hair. I had not yet poured my coffee; I was in my pajamas. It was Monday; my week was as yet unformed. By noon, my daughter, who is almost seven, announced I had pulled eighty-seven lice from her head. I do not think her counting was careful, but it is indisputable that there were many, many bugs. The literature on head lice refers to this as a "neglected infestation."

There was an epidemic in her school, but the administration had failed to notify families. On the Saturday before we found the louse, my daughter told me her head was itchy. "It's the pool chlorine," I told her, with misleading motherly certainty. "We have to wash your hair better after swim lessons. We have to find you a good conditioner." I placed the blame squarely on "we." "We," like the passive voice, implicates no one in particular. I had neglected to do anything helpful. I didn't know that insects lurked on her scalp, feeding off her blood.

I was fretting about the virus inching closer by the minute from both continental Europe and the jagged line of the West Coast. I had already filled a large Tupperware bin with lentils and Annie's macaroni and cheese and dried mangos—the pantry staples of the bourgeoisie, not a tinned vegetable in sight. In early February, when the disease still seemed very far away, I had read that children's bodies bore the virus well. I had breathed out my fear on behalf of other, far-away parents; I didn't realize then that I would be implicated in this relative good news. But now, weeks later, I was worried about my community—the old, the vulnerable—because scientists and public health experts said I should be. Also, these same scientists noted that not enough people were worried, and I like to be in the minority. I called my aging, immunosuppressed parents and asked them to hole up in the woods and allow my sister to buy them groceries. Anxiety—and titillation—were growing inside me: this was strange and different. This was frightening and interesting.

The lice were not interesting. They were a logistical nightmare.

My husband had to teach a morning class. The pharmacy, which is across the street from the plagued school, was nearly out of lice products; only a few dusty and scuffed off-brand packages remained. (The hand sanitizer and soap were already long gone.) The options were undesirable, but I returned to my family with a chemical plan in hand.

Back home, my daughter shed her pajamas recklessly, with no respect for best lice-eradication practices; she lolled on the couch cushions. My toddler could not abide the attention I was lavishing upon his older sister's head. Bored by the minuscule parameters offered by the pink bathroom walls, he whined, he moaned. He wanted me to comb his hair, to douse him with the poisonous spray that did not, in fact, kill the lice instantly, as advertised—no, they simply waded through it across her scalp! In desperation I went to the attic and produced a bag of giant cardboard building blocks and a honking rubber pig. The toddler did not care for either. After an hour of his wails, I came to my senses and put on the television. He sat for the rest of the morning in a dull torpor as I worked my way through strands of my daughter's dark blond hair and pulled out bug after bug after godforsaken bug, filling the toilet with them.

There was, of course, a lone louse on him, so he got the nit comb and the spray after all, as requested. As it turned out, he didn't care for that either.

There were seven nits on the nape of my own neck. My husband pulled them off my hair in a kind of tender, unerotic act of care that felt like a harbinger of marriage's best-case endgame.

The lice filled me with dread. I could not shake the image of my daughter's head as it wriggled with bugs. Horror movies and grisly detective procedurals have taught me that bodies covered in bugs are typically dead. That lesson clung to me like a nit, even as I sat in the sun of my bathroom window and held my daughter's warm, alive head in my hands. Frantically navigating the lice chores—laundry, vacuuming, combing—I felt miserable and afraid. Lice do not kill you, nor do they make you sick. I was afraid, however, that they would never leave. I was afraid that I had failed her.

My daughter missed school that Monday. She spent the afternoon wearing a shower cap over a head doused in fairly high-quality olive oil. It was unseasonably warm and she cavorted on the porch, alongside the toddler who was likewise wearing a "silly hat!!!"

"We have lice!" she announced to the neighbors. (I could not help wishing that I had been offered the same courtesy—a piercing announcement—by her school.) A few minutes later another set of neighbors ambled past: universities and offices were open, coffee shops were selling coffee. "We have lice!" she told them, too. They stopped to commiserate but kept their distance. Who wants lice?

By Friday her school was closing to quell the spread of coronavirus. She returned home with packet after packet of dull worksheets.

"I will be homeschooled now," she announced. I noted her use of the passive voice. Our agency was removed from the situation.

THAT WEEK, as it became more apparent that life was going to unravel in huge and frightening ways, my husband and I took turns each night pulling glistening nits from my daughter's hair, dragging them with our fingernails along the strands upon which they had made their home. At first she was agreeable and accommodating, vacuuming the sofa after a nit-picking session, reveling in hours of television and in the French braids that I was finally mastering, after years of requests. But as the week wore on her goodwill thinned and she wept.

My expertise in contagion grew in inverse relation to her patience: lice live off a head for not much more than twenty-four hours. The coronavirus survives on plastic for up to three days; its life on a wooden surface is shorter. Lice do not fly, but they crawl speedily. The coronavirus's incubation period is two weeks—unless it isn't; experts disagree. Nits alone do not indicate an infestation, because not all nits will hatch. I considered how long it takes for a nit to hatch into a louse (seven to ten days), and how long it takes for COVID-19 to replicate and expand and fill someone's body with discomfort, misery, and then, perhaps, death (four days to several weeks). *Don't let the bugs keep you up,* my older and wiser sister advised via text.

The school closure will kill the lice. The children have carried the bugs and their eggs home, where they are almost certainly passing them back and forth between their siblings; but ultimately an adult in each household will vanquish the family infestation, pulling the final nit from the last strand of hair. This complete triumph would be impossible if the children continued to lean together over *Ivy & Bean* inside their brightly lit classroom, to roll like puppies on the spongy surface of the playground.

But whereas nits are small and countable, a particle of coronavirus is microscopic and nebulous: the schools darken and lock up, but still the virus wafts forward, infinitely for all we know, until perhaps something stops it. We hope.

ON THURSDAY, the night before the schools closed, we found two more bugs. I was crushed. I felt as if I were losing my kid to them, that they had rendered her contagious and unhuggable.

I was, by this time, angry that the schools had not already shuttered. But I was not worried that she or the toddler would become ill from COVID-19. I was not worried that they would die; I knew that, in the grand scheme of things, my children were safe. I took solace in the numbers. I *was* afraid for my parents. I felt haunted watching our elderly neighbors drink their coffee on the front steps, inspecting their daffodils with proprietary pride.

On Thursday, however, as I watched the second round of lice wriggle under the flashlight of my cell phone, in the warm, low light of the living room, I felt newly afraid.

It was, I think, the repulsiveness—the fundamental wrongness—of the second generation of bugs on her head that somehow invited the contemplation of both her mortality, which is a path I try to avoid traversing, and the impossibility of stopping a plague. I had been so careful, *and yet*. The two bugs seemed to have arrived to remind me of both my daughter's vulnerability, and the terrifying laws of contagion: I could do everything right—shampoo, comb, vacuum, wash and dry, braid, spray—and still the bugs could grow and multiply and skitter from head to head. It only took one live egg.

On Monday, my worry about COVID-19 had been gaseous and thin. It was vague and peppered with intrigue. What should I do? What will happen? *How bad will this get?*

But when the lice returned, my fear of the virus thickened, filled my throat. I still do not believe that it will kill my children, but the tiny, sand-colored bugs rendered visible the coronavirus's ability to multiply with ease, in spite of our best efforts; what would I do if I feared that something so wily could truly harm her?

I have spent the last weeks in a state of uncertain caution:

Should I walk with a friend if we remain six feet apart? Should the children bike in the park? Should we get takeout? Should we open the postbox to mail this letter? Should I wipe down my credit card after using it to buy groceries?

I am almost never sure that I have made the right decision: I could always have been more careful. I cleaned my wallet with rubbing alcohol after the grocery store, but I let the credit card fester. If my daughter's warm, scabbed head were in mortal danger, I would have swabbed the card, my keys, everything—all without hesitation. I don't wish that it had come for the children, this novel coronavirus. But would things be different if it had?

None of us know when or how this will end; how the failures, large and small, will destroy and rearrange lives. I can see kids scooting and skateboarding in the park outside my bedroom window. They look happy enough—schools are pretty tedious institutions, after all—but they may not fare so well when all is said and done.

My worry simmers. The element of titillation has seeped out of the pandemic: people near me sicken, and lose lifelines (income, access to others). A friend's wife has a baby alone; partners are no longer allowed in the hospital. In the photos she holds both a newborn and an iPad, her smile concealed by a mask. My daughter looks over at my phone—we are together now, all day long—and I stuff the phone between the couch cushions: I do not want her to see this.

The lice are gone now, I think. They were terrible, but also fine; the logistical challenges that once seemed all consuming are already irrelevant—dwarfed, even, by new impossibilities. The bugs came and I killed them, but they left me with the nausea of seeing someone I love threatened by a random, predatory force.

Spring

Maya C. Popa

Time persists, yes, I can see there are new branches.

The grass, first in a line of transformations,
seemingly risen overnight.

Color is pouring back into the hours,
or forgiveness, whatever the case may be.

With one decisive tug at the earth, the robin's drawn forth
a shimmering worm,

with such precision, it is almost a cruel pleasure.

This, the nightmare we dreamed but did not wake from.

Time is passing, I concede. A squirrel leaps
from one branch to another.

A hawk studies the field at dusk.

The park announces the season over and over
to no one,

and the silence cranes to listen.

Terraces of light now that the day is longer.

When joy comes, will I be ready, I wonder.

APRIL

Memories of West Fourth Street

Major Jackson

Why right now is the iridescent blue of that bird
from our walk above Villa Montalvo
coming to me like an omen? I look back
and hear Plato talking to himself about futures
by a cluster of eucalyptus trees. Why right now
this cosmic skullduggery (or kindheartedness? I can't tell)
on a train platform, some wild chief big longhair type
running Monk's scales? The tune? *Don't Blame Me.*
The swiftest blood-hold when a woman performed
an adjacent stomp and fanned her arms as if beckoning
infinite light drifting from commuters
hastening home like Vikings. At times, it felt as if
I were being disrobed in public, sliding like a glyph
beneath the melody of a man trying to put a few steaks
on his table, but what was really going down
between the departures and arrivals?
I was the next broken beauty, carved by a groove.
I was human and hungry and prosperous.

The Law of *Salus Populi*

John Fabian Witt

"Salus populi suprema lex," wrote Cicero: "The health of the people is the supreme law." For at least two thousand years, lawyers and statesmen have insisted that the public's health supersedes the ordinary processes of law and politics, and never more so than in times of emergency. The idea is at once hopeful and dangerous. Cicero's dictum imagines reassuringly that we will be able to escape the usual messy afflictions of the body politic and accomplish what the crisis necessitates. But suspending existing laws and institutions also threatens to undo the hard-won protections of our rights. Martial law or even dictatorship looms, unbound by existing legal restraints.

The history of public health emergencies in the United States, however, shows that crises do not create a state of exception, nor do they beget radically new beginnings, with all their possibilities and perils. For better and for worse, past American public health emergencies have reproduced the preexisting patterns and practices of law and politics, with all the vices and perhaps some of the virtues those patterns entail, reinforcing rather than revising the major themes of American life.

Modern North American history begins with an infectious disease crisis, when Eurasian germs arrived on the continent beginning in the late fifteenth century. In 1492, an estimated 2 million people lived in North America east of the Mississippi River. But European contact literally decimated this native population, mostly thanks to diseases like smallpox and measles. By 1750, only around a quarter million Native Americans remained.

In their own communities, settler and colonial authorities built institutions to limit the toll of disease. The Massachusetts Bay Colony established quarantines for vessels when yellow fever broke out in Barbados in the 1640s. And soon after American independence, a yellow fever epidemic chased President George Washington out of Philadelphia, then the capital, and led the city's authorities to establish a board of health. For the next century, state and local health commissions exercised broad powers to quarantine the sick, to condemn unsanitary properties, to exclude infectious and potentially infectious immigrants, and to compel vaccination for diseases like smallpox. In the name of "the life and health of . . . citizens," as two prominent officials put it at the end of the nineteenth century, such commissions coerced "the ignorant, the selfish, the careless and the vicious."

By many accounts, state and local interventions—coercive or otherwise—were remarkably successful at stopping the spread of disease. New York established the Metropolitan Board of Health in 1866, with sweeping authority to clean the streets, collect and record information about infections, disinfect infected properties, and even go door to door to wipe out unsanitary practices. Diseases like cholera were essentially eradicated. As the University of Michigan historian William Novak puts it in *The People's Welfare,* a classic book on the subject, American public health efforts embodied "a vigorous conception of the regulatory powers of the state." State and local governments deployed fast, flexible responses—federal authorities played almost no role in early public health administration—responses that were increasingly informed by professional expertise. Public health professionals expelled disease after disease, ensuring that yellow fever, smallpox, and other pestilential diseases no longer acted as terrible scourges in American life. A century later, we benefit every day from the work of the first great public health effort.

Health experts relied on what nineteenth-century jurists often called the power of "overruling necessity"—essentially, the authority to do whatever was required to preserve human welfare. But "overruling necessity" did not overthrow the ordinary institutions of American law. Instead, public health imperatives activated those institutions and set them into motion. Throughout the nineteenth century, Americans went to court to challenge the authority of new public health authorities to condemn property, impose quarantines, compel vaccination, and more. Judges reviewed such public health regulations for reasonableness in the same way they reviewed executive and legislative action of virtually all kinds. Courts generally upheld the actions of health authorities, but they insisted that regulation bear a rational relationship to an actual health imperative, and judges made clear that they had the final authority to determine whether a crisis existed and what measures were permitted. As one New York judge put it in *People v. Roff,* an 1856 quarantine case, public health crises did not "suspend the operation of the constitution" or allow the state to infringe "all the natural rights of the citizen." The most important public health crisis case in American history, *Jacobson v. Massachusetts,* decided by the Supreme Court in 1905, upheld a mandatory vaccination program that aimed to slow an outbreak of smallpox in Cambridge, Massachusetts. But even here, the Court noted that the state could not compel vaccination in "an arbitrary, unreasonable manner."

Of course, ordinary law brought with it all-too-ordinary discriminations and injustices. Interventions to stop the spread of cholera from the 1830s through the 1860s regularly targeted poor, Irish, and

largely Catholic neighborhoods. During the Civil War and Recon-
struction, the dislocation resulting from emancipation touched off
a smallpox scourge among freedpeople to which medical authorities
gave little if any attention. Sanitary commission efforts to compel
vaccination scapegoated poor, Jewish, and eastern European communities. (Officials took it for granted, as one wrote bluntly, that
"the death-rate of a particular ward or block" would vary "with the
poverty of its inhabitants" by between "ten to fifteen years.") Authorities in places like San Francisco ruthlessly discriminated against
people of Chinese descent in the effort to stem the spread of the
plague at the turn of the twentieth century. In the Southwest, officials
adopted pseudo-scientific regulations that produced and entrenched
racial status hierarchies. Under Jim Crow, public health authorities
typically treated infectious disease in Black communities only when
outbreaks threatened to spread across the tracks to the white side of
town. Gay men beset by the HIV/AIDS crisis in the 1980s and 1990s
had to launch a fierce social mobilization to win the attention and
care of their government. At the turn of the twenty-first century,
the best epidemiology estimated that 10 percent of the difference in
mortality between Blacks and whites was attributable to infectious
disease.

Today a new set of challenges confronts the health of the people,
but the basic legal landscape is familiar. Federal quarantine orders
would be relatively novel and legally uncertain, but state and local
orders to shelter in place and mandatory quarantines are not new
innovations at odds with our historic civil liberties. Citizens accustomed to a century and more of freedom from the "overruling necessity" of public health restrictions may be surprised to learn that local
officials can arrest them for defying orders to shelter in place. Such
orders are among the most traditional modes of government action.

These early days of the novel coronavirus crisis replicate the patterns that left us so unprepared for it in the first place. A callous and supremely self-interested president governs, as he always has, with a cunning instinct for political success and the maturity of an angry toddler. He leads a political party that has been committed to starving the federal government and minimizing its health care capacity for decades. A market-based health care system with a just-in-time model of patient care has left us without critical reserves, even as the business lobby and the White House dither over invoking the much-needed Defense Production Act. As the federal government cedes the field, a hodgepodge of state and local institutions, decentralized hospitals, and private industry scrambles to patch together a response that is alternately inspiring and inadequate. Unjustifiable racial and economic inequalities decide who lives and who dies. Just as they always have.

Meanwhile, the political debates breaking out among people living in isolation or in quarantine proceed according to script, replicating the bitter polarization of a year ago, or two years ago, or three. There are debates over abortion, race and sex inequalities, class injustice, civil liberties, mass incarceration, and immigration controls, now filtered through the provision of medical care. In crisis, the fault lines of ordinary politics reappear, only now they are deeper.

The real supreme law is not our health but our fecklessness—tempered by institutions that have sometimes managed to redeem us nonetheless.

Pandemic Inequality

Octávio Luiz Motta Ferraz

As I entered the third week of self-isolation in my home in East London, news of the first death from COVID-19 in Rio de Janeiro arrived on my smartphone. She was a sixty-three-year-old woman, a domestic servant, caring for her boss. The boss had just returned from a holiday in Italy, where she was infected with the virus. Like many wealthy Brazilians, the boss must have seen nothing wrong with "self-isolating" but still requiring that her servant come to work. For the domestic worker, self-isolation was, of course, never an option. "If you don't come to work, you don't get paid"—as simple as that. The case offers a stark example of the perverse interaction between pandemics and inequalities. Depending on the scale of inequalities in your society—the *real* social distance—and where you stand economically, your chances of riding out a pandemic will vary significantly. The poorer you are, the worse your prospects will be.

As is now well known, pandemics are not equal opportunity events. The poor bear a disproportionate burden of morbidity and mortality because of three overlapping and reinforcing disadvantages caused by poverty: differential exposure, differential susceptibility, and differential access to health care. Differential exposure results mainly from unfavorable living conditions (overcrowding, lack of access to sanitation and clean water) but also from adverse working conditions (lack of paid sick leave, lack of protective equipment) and lack of education about how to avoid risky behavior—if possible. Differential susceptibility derives from worse underlying health conditions associated with poverty, such as malnutrition, psychological stress, high blood pressure, diabetes, and heart disease. Differential access to health care, caused by lack of private insurance, limited access to public services, or the inability to adhere to treatment, completes the triad of disadvantage. In short, the poor are more exposed and susceptible to disease, less capable of accessing health care when they catch it, and thus more likely to pass it on.

Previous pandemics have provided plenty of evidence of this negative feedback loop. The HIV/AIDS pandemic provides a sobering illustration. Its 32 million deaths and 75 million infections so far have disproportionately burdened the poorest across and within countries. Of the 37.9 million people currently living with HIV across the world, more than one-third, most of them from Western and Central Africa, Asia, and the Pacific, have no access to antiretrovirals. The vast majority of the 1.7 million new infections still occurring every year take place in poor countries or poor areas within rich ones. In the United States, HIV prevalence among the urban poor is 2.1 percent, more than double the 1 percent cutoff that defines a generalized HIV epidemic such as those found in badly affected poor countries like Burundi, Ethiopia, Angola, and Haiti.

What is true of HIV/AIDS is also the case with other pandemics. To cite just one other example much more similar to COVID-19, studies have shown that in the United Kingdom the 2009–2010 H1N1 influenza killed three times more people among the poorest 20 percent than among the richest 20 percent.

We can expect socioeconomic inequalities to keep playing a decisive role in how the current pandemic develops everywhere. Here in the United Kingdom, the curse of inequality was plain during the first days of the quarantine. Many were surprised to see the London Underground teeming with people the day after the prime minister's television address on March 23 urging everyone to stay at home. A survey of 2,108 U.K. adults brought to light the obvious explanation: only 44 percent reported being able to work from home. Ability to do so varied significantly between managerial and professional workers (60 percent) and manual, semi-skilled, and casual workers (19 percent). It goes without saying that those whose employment doesn't allow working from home also tend to be the lowest paid. During the 2009–2010 H1N1 epidemic, which killed more than twelve thousand Americans, three in ten U.S. workers with symptoms continued going to work despite social-distancing advice, driving 27 percent of all infections.

The U.K. government did realize, albeit belatedly, that mere pleas for "social distancing" would not work under such circumstances, finally adding to its crisis package a grant to help millions of low-paid self-employed people who were unsure how to quarantine and put food on the table at the same time. But the help is arriving only in early June—a wait many cannot afford, just as millions of poor Americans now face a delay in getting the $1,200 stimulus pay from the U.S. Congress's emergency aid package of March 27. The burden on the limited unemployment benefits system in the United Kingdom has already been felt, with nearly a million new claims made in just two weeks (ten times more than the average). In the United States, claims for unemployment benefits also surged, from 282,000 to 6.6 million over two weeks.

In less affluent and more unequal societies the problem is much more complex and dramatic. In overcrowded living conditions such as in the favelas of Brazil, where many domestic servants and other low-paid workers and the unemployed live, the prospects are the worst possible. In the despairing words of Gilson Rodrigues, a community leader in Paraisópolis, the largest favela of São Paulo: "It is here that we will have more cases [of COVID-19], in the favelas. How can an old person self-isolate in a house with ten people and two rooms? This isolation is a joke; it is for the rich. The poor cannot do it. We are going to lose a lot of people in the favelas, sadly."

I heard similar outrage from my friend Leonardo, self-quarantined in Rocinha (Rio de Janeiro), the largest favela in Latin America. "The TV in Brazil thinks everyone is rich," he complained. "They offer tips on how not to gain weight during the quarantine! On how to use the playground of the gated condo safely! Here in the favela people will not stay inside. When the hunger hits things will become tragic."

Compounding the problems of lack of income and cramped accommodation of the 13.6 million people who live in favelas in Brazil, most lack access to basic sanitation, and many suffer from constant interruptions in water supply. It is hard to envisage how people living under such conditions will be able to follow quarantine measures when even washing hands is a struggle. According to a recent survey of 1,142 residents of 262 favelas across Brazil, 86 percent would not be able to withstand a month of quarantine without going hungry.

The Brazilian political establishment has not remained totally oblivious to the impending calamity. After much negotiation, a grant of R$600 (U.S.$115, 60 percent of the minimum wage) was approved by the lower house of the Congress for a period of three months for those unable to earn above a certain threshold due to the COVID-19 crisis. Yet this money will not buy much, and considering the inevitable difficulties and delays in getting it to those who need it, it is likely to at best minimize the suffering.

There are more dramatic cases than the Brazilian one, such as the situation in India, with its forty-five thousand stranded migrant workers. But everywhere, with varying degrees of intensity, the negative feedback loop between the pandemic and inequality will show its ugly face.

As I brace myself for another week of quarantine, I crave not only the end of the crisis but discussion and implementation of the lessons we may learn from it. Unless we significantly diminish the stark social distance that separates us in normal times, each new pandemic will prove that we are not, in fact, all in this together.

The Pandemic in Inupiaq

Joan Naviyuk Kane

It's nice to impart a piece of good news. On the phone, I'm telling my mother about our King Island dictionary, which we've almost finished digitizing.

"But," my twelve-year-old son interjects, "we were getting kicked out of Mom's office building—they almost didn't let us in on the last day! I have to fix the page order and put it in a PDF again."

It's 9 p.m. in Cambridge, Massachusetts, and my younger son, who turned ten last month, is sitting on the living room floor of our apartment eating a bowl of rice. I've called my parents in Anchorage, in part to check on them, in part so my mom can ask the boys when they're going to bed, in part so the boys can thank her for the letters they received (in which she asked my younger son, "Why do you stay up so long?").

And I called in part to ask my mother about Inupiaq etymology. King Island is where our family is from. When I moved to Cambridge to take a yearlong fellowship at the Radcliffe Institute, one of my projects—one I hoped to share with my sons—was completing a dictionary of the dialect we grew up speaking. I'm trying to find a word for *pandemic*. The etymology in English is muddied, and semantic vagueness troubles me. I see people using a cognate—*Sikpin?*—for "Are you sick?" but it doesn't seem right. I find words in other dialects that don't seem to have affinity with words in the King Island dialect.

I ask my mom about the prefix *naŋ-*. It seems to have to do with avoidance, precarity, suffering, speaking ill, inflicting pain. *Naŋaagaa:* She/he is avoiding it. *Naŋiikłaa:* She/he is complaining about her/him. *Naŋiaġna.tuq:* A precipitous place is frightening. *Naŋiaqtuŋa:* I feel terror in a precarious place. *Naŋiituq:* She/he is sick. *Naŋitkia:* She/he beat her/him. *Naŋiirvik:* hospital, sanatorium. *Naŋirun* translates to "epidemic" in most Inupiaq dialects. My mother's explanation is characteristically direct: "It's something that makes you suffer. Naŋirun."

I tell my mom that my older son and I have been experiencing a lot of déjà vu. Tonight he helped me make an eggplant and potato curry with ingredients from a combination of sources—none of them a grocery store. He was eager to mince garlic once we'd trimmed spots of rot; he watched me peel a ginger root before taking on the task himself. When he tastes the finished dish, then asks if we can make it again tomorrow without the eggplant, I stop and tell him I feel like we've had this conversation before.

"Me, too. But I've never been brave or hungry enough to try eggplant until tonight," he answers.

"Déjà vu," I explain.

"Like when I hear a Brahms concerto for the first time but it feels like I'm remembering it," he says.

"Like my dreams when I wake up in the morning," says his younger brother.

So many quotidian aspects of our day are marked with the way they feel familiar, are familiar, and yet are things we experience anew. I wonder how much of the way our memories work, how our feeling of having already seen or lived through our extant experiences are shaped by the historical trauma and epigenetic methylation of my maternal grandmother having been orphaned in the 1918 flu pandemic.

Our phone calls with my mother punctuate the days now. My sons record words in our dialect and learn to make sentences. They ask her questions. We don't speak of the future, and I don't want to ask too much about her mother. My grandmother's parents and three siblings were all killed by the flu at Qawairaq (Mary's Igloo) on the Seward Peninsula where, according to ethnohistorians, the mortality rate was 54 percent. I don't ask about the baby boy who died, according to church records, at the orphanage where my grandmother and her two sisters were raised through early childhood.

Instead, we talk about things she might remember from her visits to Harvard Square twenty, twenty-five years ago, when I was an undergraduate and she was the proud mother of the first Inupiaq bound to take a degree at Harvard College. We tell her about the empty streets of Cambridge and Boston. Of the boys sharing one scooter, using the bike lanes to get around now that there's no traffic. We report on the birds and blooms we catalogue on our daily walks.

I tell her about the Inuit-related books I've managed to read lately. I tell her how I spend hours teaching my younger son long division. Helping the boys with Spanish, Mandarin, social studies, and a dozen other subjects. I say we're playing violin duets and flute trios together. I spare her the details of the essay I am trying to write, the one I need to step away from in order to sleep.

The essay I started to write reads as a complaint, a summary of injustices, a preparation for worse to come. I think of the federal termination of the Mashpee Wampanoag tribe's rights to sovereign land that has just happened in the past few days, the government removing their land from the trust status that protected it. I think of the eighty-one ventilators—eighty-one—the Indian Health Service is said to have for all of us beneficiaries of the system.

I hope my parents stay home. I hope people stay away from them. We're so far from them, with no way of returning to Alaska and no place to stay even if we did. My sons like it here in Massachusetts, though they dream of moving to Abu Dhabi, to Japan, maybe spending a couple of years in the E.U.

In recent weeks we've all stopped saying things like "Remember when we had a house?" or "I miss having a yard." My sons now say, "I miss my friends." I ask which friends, in Alaska or Cambridge? "All of them," they say. Cambridge is empty. Our building is almost vacant. We're stuck here for now.

We moved away from Alaska for Massachusetts last August, several weeks ahead of schedule. Wells Fargo had begun posting notices on our family home that the bank would soon be boarding up the doors and windows. A judge had ordered me to stop paying the mortgage (which I'd qualified for as a tribally enrolled home buyer), determining it was my ex-husband's responsibility. He hadn't paid for more than eight months.

My sons and I spent most of the spring and summer emptying out the house, sorting our belongings into one of three piles: ship, share, sell. I can't remember what we did with the N95 respirator masks. They had become a necessity in our final weeks as we ferried boxes to the post office, brought bin after bin to relatives or Goodwill. I confer with my sons: they tell me we tossed the masks into the garbage before boarding our redeye to Seattle.

Anchorage's hospitals had been handing out the masks to patients as a matter of public health. Air quality in much of Alaska had been deemed hazardous for most of the summer as six hundred wildfires burned areas roughly equal in size to the state of Connecticut. Millions of acres of the state's trees were dead of an infestation of invasive spruce-bark beetles; the invasion had spread as decades of dramatically rising temperatures expanded their habitat. Forests stood tinder-dry after prolonged drought. Many months in 2018 and 2019 saw the hottest days in the history of recorded subarctic and arctic temperatures; Anchorage had a newsworthy stretch of ninety-degree days in early July.

The state was ill prepared to contain these wildfires—some caused by humans, some sparked by lightning, more prevalent in the intensifying storms of the arctic and subarctic—having never invested much in training or educating its population. Much of Alaska continues to do without running water, roads, and communications networks.

In Anchorage—a racist, violent city already in financial crisis due to Alaska's dependence on petroleum and colonial economic policies, compounded by a massive 7.1 earthquake in November 2018—office buildings, schools, homes, and hospitals lacked air-filtration systems that could make the air safe to breathe. It was a relief to dump those masks in the trash on our way out: reminders of the multiple traumas we were leaving.

We left a place that was not healthy. We adapted. We adjusted our expectations of time, space, and one another.

Have the governments imposed upon my family—municipal, state, and federal—ever responded constructively to disasters? Or have they only perpetuated them, protracted them? How much trust could I have?

When I wake my older son, he asks if he can read the news before he reads a book. I consent. I wish I knew how other single mothers cope right now with schools shut, child care programs on hiatus, and the libraries, bookstores, and playgrounds closed to everyone. I've found little relief from the constant work of parenting, teaching my students, keeping house, and helping my sons stay up to date with school between cooking, cleaning, corresponding with students and my bosses at two different universities, trying to find a job to carry us beyond the end of my fellowship year. I can't bring myself to respond to most emails and texts. I call my parents. I wish I could tell my sons something certain.

I consider the stretch ahead: how much closer we might grow, how clear our boundaries might become. We're fortunate to weather this here. We read. I write much less than I hope to. I wonder when things will change. As an indigenous woman subject to the legacy of hundreds of years of genocide and disease from settler colonizers and their agents, and subject in my lifetime to the ever-present apparatus of American systems, I wonder if things have ever stopped changing for my family—for my mother, for my sons. For my community. I think about our changing, living language, too. What do I convey to my children?

Naguasautuq: It got better? *Itqiitigaaŋa:* It makes me uneasy. *Agulaq:* It is the distance between things.

A Nurse Comes to Brooklyn

Nell Freudenberger

When Donna Flint was a child in Little Rock, she loved science fiction. Her father was a paramedic, then a firefighter, and they watched medical shows like *ER* together, as well as *Star Wars* and *Star Trek*—Flint was especially interested in the futuristic technology used in the sickbay. She grew up wanting to be an ER doctor, hoping to work in the most intense part of the hospital and save lives under pressure. Then, she told me, "life happened." She got pregnant when she was eighteen and had a daughter, an experience that sharpened her life to a hard point. "I was a single mom. I didn't go to nursing school until later in life. As a single parent raising a child and working, it was—" she hesitated and then laughed, "quite the task."

Flint decided that she wanted her daughter to go to private school. She needed money for tuition, and was always looking for opportunities; at Walmart, where she worked for eight years, she started as a cashier and gradually moved up the ladder to supervise overseas shipping. She was chosen for a management training program, but a friend convinced her to take an inventory control job with better benefits at Dassault Falcon, a private jet manufacturer. In 2008, after she was laid off during the financial crisis, she started putting herself through nursing school, working on the side as a nanny and then a student nurse tech. In school, she said, she fell in love with the heart. "I just liked that system the best of the body. Your body is designed to compensate. In a lot of ways, the body is designed to heal itself. When the heart has issues—if there's a blocked vessel or something—there's all these compensatory mechanisms, where the vasculature will reroute to get the heart what it needs, so that it can supply the blood for your body. I just always found those kinds of things fascinating." She learned cardiac telemetry, which measures a patient's respiratory rate, oxygen saturation, and the electrical activity of the heart, but it wasn't only the technology that compelled her. The heart was its own astonishingly complex machine, able to adapt when threatened.

When her daughter Brianna, now nineteen, left Little Rock for college this year, Flint said, "I just felt lost. I'd raised this kid since I was eighteen. And I'd been responsible, and I just felt like *Well, what do I do with myself now?*" She'd been thinking about the possibilities, and had considered medical missionary work. She'd always wanted to travel, and although she'd once worked for a luxury aircraft company, she'd never been on a flight herself. Then the pandemic hit, and her daughter returned to Little Rock.

At the end of March, New York governor Andrew Cuomo put out a nationwide all-call for doctors and nurses. Normally a state license is required to practice nursing in New York, but the city had waived it because of the crisis, and Flint thought this might be serendipity. "I'm not a risk taker," she told me. "I'm a safe-bet kind of girl. But I said, *You know what? I'm gonna just do it.*" She put in an application with a recruiter and got an offer immediately. Her daughter was more than capable of taking care of the house and their dogs while she was gone. Flint said that although she'd gotten used to putting herself last, "this time I just decided to do something for me, that I wanted to do, no matter what whoever thought about it." And what she wanted to do for herself was to come to a Brooklyn hospital and treat patients with coronavirus.

I met Flint one night on the sidewalk outside our house. My husband and I live in Park Slope with our two children half a block from Brooklyn Methodist Hospital, which recently became an arm of NewYork-Presbyterian and has been undergoing expansion and renovation. Before construction began, some of our neighbors circulated a petition to stop it, concerned that our leafy block of brownstones would become a staging area for heavy machinery, the relative quiet shattered by cement mixers and jackhammers. That didn't sound great to us either, but we couldn't bring ourselves to sign the petition; the hospital had been so important in our lives already. Our son, who suffered episodes of croup as an infant, was diagnosed with asthma at three. He'd been born with a mild form of hemophilia, and the combination of two disorders that might require immediate medical attention at any time made having the hospital so close enormously comforting. We had needed to run him down the block to the pediatric ER in the middle of the night several times, and on one occasion spent three nights at the hospital. Once the 7 p.m. appreciation for health care workers started in March, we were out on our stoop every night, clapping.

The kids noticed Flint first, maybe because of her precision timing. She appeared on the block almost every evening between 7:00 and 7:05. She wore dark blue scrubs, a green surgical mask, a flowered scarf over her hair, and a black-and-white–striped backpack. She was short and compact with a round, young-looking face, smooth brown skin, and a determined way of walking up the hill. Some of the nurses, and many of the doctors, pass by without looking during the evening applause; they seem very tired or sometimes embarrassed by the attention. Flint was different. You could tell she was smiling, even underneath the mask. She was like a celebrity to the children, "There she is!" they cried as soon as we spotted her coming down the block. Sometimes she was on the phone, but she always waved and made eye contact.

We got into the habit of leaving our stoop and going up to the corner across the street from the hospital where a small crowd gathered every evening to applaud. Blue buses honked as they went by, the phrase "I [heart] New York" lit up on their LED screens in place of a destination. One neighbor blew a bugle, another shook a tambourine, and another played percussion with two tennis rackets that he beat on lidded city recycling cans. One night the kids ran ahead in their masks and pajamas, and I walked next to Flint on the narrow sidewalk, inevitably a little closer than we were supposed to be. She thanked us for clapping; I said it was the least we could do. "Where are you coming from?" I asked. I only meant to inquire about her commute—I was wondering if she had to take the subway to get to the hospital. "I'm here from Little Rock," she said.

Flint agreed to talk with me about her motivations for coming to Brooklyn, and one morning at 9, after her shift ended, we talked via FaceTime for over an hour. I kept offering to let her go, aware that she'd been up all night, but she wasn't planning to sleep yet. "I'm a talker," she said, laughing. "Can you tell?" I realized when we got off that I had forgotten to ask what to me was an important question: arriving in Brooklyn as she had at a time when the city had the highest infection rate of anywhere in the world, going into the ICU— where the normal nurse-to-patient ratio of one to two had ballooned to one-to-five or even one-to-six critically ill patients—was she afraid? I texted her, and she wrote back: "Just being completely honest the first day I saw the ICU I was! Not scared in the sense that I could not do the work. I am confident in my abilities . . . but I was scared of the course of the disease in the patients. More a fear of the unknown.

I don't think it crossed my mind to be afraid for myself when I looked at all of the people that were extremely sick. I do feel the emotion of it all but I have been told that one of my special talents is staying patient, having a calm demeanor, and keeping a level head when situations are very stressful and chaotic. My whole life I have always had to be strong."

NewYork-Presbyterian had given Flint a choice of a four-, eight-, or thirteen-week contract. She chose the longest. "I can do anything for three months," she said. She arrived on April 13, at the tail end of the worst devastation. In a hospital that had, prior to COVID-19, typically supported an average of twenty patients on ventilators, there were now six times that number. Flint was sometimes juggling three patients on multiple medications, "just back and forth, back and forth, between hanging things and starting this or that, and then, heaven forbid, a patient codes." I asked Flint what happened if two of her patients coded—experienced cardiopulmonary arrest—at the same time, and she said, "Exactly." Due to the severity of the virus, critical care nurses were in high demand, and the hospital had been forced to hastily train other nurses to support them. Many of them were working overtime. By the time Flint got there, the hospital had enough personal protective equipment, but during the worst period the nurses had been asked to reuse their soiled masks and gowns. "My first week I was like, *Jesus Christ, this is insanity.* It was very, very overwhelming."

Shortly after she arrived, a friend from Little Rock joined her, and the two women shared an apartment on the ground floor of a brownstone that they'd rented through Airbnb. Her friend, who was working uptown at Columbia Presbyterian, said that the other nurses there "kind of suggested that they didn't wear their badges on the way to work" for fear of being targeted. Flint's daughter had read on the internet about attacks on nurses—she'd even heard of a health care worker in the Philippines being doused with bleach—and she was worried about her mom. Flint said, "Some of my friends back home say, 'I've heard that in New York, you all are killing people.' It's appalling to think that, but I said, 'Well, not at my hospital.'"

In spite of those stories, Flint always got dressed in her scrubs at the apartment and wore her badge on the short walk to the hospital so that she was ready when she arrived. She worked mostly with the same group of ICU nurses, many of whom had been there through the worst part of the crisis, "showing up to work every day, day in and day out . . . toughing it out the whole month that this has been going on before all the help started to arrive." The doctors impressed her too, stepping in to do jobs that normally belonged to nurses: turning patients in their beds or bringing them pillows. In the past, she acknowledged, she'd known doctors who were high-handed, seemingly too busy to answer questions, but that wasn't the case now. "They will jump in and get their hands dirty."

Many of Flint's patients are intubated, and sedated to keep them comfortable. When they are awake, communication can be difficult because of the tube. Flint remembers one man in particular, notable to everyone in the ICU because he was recovering. None of the communication boards that patients use to convey their needs were available, so Flint wrote the alphabet on a piece of paper so the patient could tell her what he wanted. He made her laugh by asking for chocolate fudge cake, although he'd only just graduated from a feeding tube to applesauce. "Every day I saw a little improvement. It was emotional because he was getting better." But he was also worried. When he improved enough to talk freely, he told Flint he'd been away from his job for five weeks already—would it still be there for him when he recovered? Lying in bed for that long had caused his muscles to atrophy to the point that he could do almost nothing for himself. "His appetite was coming back, but he was really worried about being able to stand, being able to walk and hold things, and just to even move his arms for anything. . . . We had a long moment one morning, he was just in tears—'How am I going to get back to doing those things?' "

MY HUSBAND AND I had symptoms of the coronavirus in March, early in its path through the city. I got sick first. It was mostly respiratory—it hurt to inhale, and sometimes I felt so short of breath that I used an albuterol inhaler my doctor had prescribed over the phone. I hadn't been able to get tested, but my doctor and I were pretty sure I had the virus. Still, I didn't quarantine myself from the kids. It just didn't seem practical.

Gradually I became obsessed with the possibility that I had made a terrible mistake. My husband had just started a new job, and in the current climate, we worried that he could lose it; he needed to be at his computer all the time. I was supervising remote school, cooking, doing the laundry, and ignoring the rest of the housework. Every day during his break my husband took the children outside to the park while I took a nap. The virus hadn't seemed to target children, even children with asthma—but what if? What if the price of relative normalcy—Dad at work, Mom present rather than scarily isolated behind a closed bedroom door—was one of them getting seriously ill? One weekend morning, after we'd finished cleaning up the breakfast dishes and the children were playing a card game on the rug, I suddenly had a moment of panic. I sank down to a squat on the kitchen floor next to the chair where my husband sat looking at his phone. Hidden from the children by the kitchen table, I started to cry quietly. My husband looked at me, alarmed. "I'm scared," I mouthed. Our eight-year-old peered through the legs of the table and spotted me. "Why is Mommy crying?" he asked.

When Flint's message appeared on my screen the other day, it occurred to me that bravery doesn't arrive suddenly, at a critical juncture, the way it does in movies. You don't have to wait for an extreme situation to see if you have it. Bravery is more like a talent, something that you practice over the course of a life. If your life hasn't asked it of you very often, a demanding moment might make you collapse in fear. But if you've been strengthening that muscle, training it, courage could be there when you need it.

FLINT HAD SEEN online videos of people clapping for health care workers, but she said she didn't believe it was real until her first night in Brooklyn. When she heard the noise, she thought a parade might be passing by; she went out to look, and found her landlady on the stoop, "just cheering, and there are people banging on pots and bottles and everything, and I was like, 'What's going on?' And she said, 'Oh— at 7:00, the streets of Brooklyn we just come to life and celebrate all you health care workers.'" The parade, it turned out, was for her.

When Flint announced she was going to Brooklyn, her family thought she was crazy. "Are you having a midlife crisis?" her brother asked. But Flint's daughter encouraged her to go. A little before 7 each evening, she called her mom in Brooklyn so she could hear the people she referred to as her mom's fan club. Flint calls our block "warrior row" because the cacophony intensifies as you approach the hospital. "Everybody cheering and rooting for you, like you're going into this battle and there is all this support for you to go and come back safely." She said that she didn't expect the applause, nor had she ever thought there was anything exceptional about her life. But now, she told her daughter, "I feel like a warrior."

Sirenland

Briallen Hopper

The sirens never stop. There are so many that I have nightmares about ambulances speeding down the street three or four abreast like chariots, wheels flying off, whips cracking, horses' mouths foaming. Then I'm jolted awake by an urgent mechanical groan, as if the driver is leaning on the horn right next to my bed. Sometimes, rarely, there seems to be a lull, and then, suddenly, a distant rising and falling line of sound. It must be a hallucination, I think; I am finally losing my mind, making sirens out of silence. But then the sound gets closer and shriller and starts to bore into my ear, and I know without a doubt that it's real.

My brain keeps translating the sirens into metaphor because it can't bear what they really mean: thousands of people are struggling to breathe. Thousands of other people are risking their lives to try to save them.

I live three blocks from Elmhurst Hospital, the public hospital in Queens that turned into a global COVID-19 epicenter overnight. New York City has the most cases on the planet, Queens has the most cases in New York, and Elmhurst Hospital has been flooded with hundreds of patients from Elmhurst, Corona, and Jackson Heights, the hardest-hit neighborhoods in the city. Witnesses describe what's happening there as a tsunami, a siege, a war zone, an apocalypse. The hospital is operating at five times its ICU capacity. Health care workers wear their masks and other personal protective equipment over and over again. Patients are cut off from everyone they love. Frantic family members call for updates and can't get through for days. Ventilators don't get freed up till somebody dies; immediately another patient is hooked up. There is no space to put all the bodies, so a refrigerator truck parked by the hospital serves as a makeshift morgue.

The need for social distancing means that I have to physically distance myself from the suffering that has flooded my neighborhood. But I don't want to be distant. I want to remember the people who had to fight for their last breaths here. The mother of a student at Queens College, where I teach. A trans activist who worked for decades to organize and care for our neighborhood's many vulnerable trans women, helping them get access to AIDS tests and immigration assistance and bailing them out of jail. The priest at my church, who preached extemporaneously in Spanish and English with equal hope and faith, and who placed a wine-dipped wafer on my tongue the week before the churches closed. All of them died last week. The sirens bring me closer to them.

Most Elmhurst residents can't #StayHome and order takeout. They are the ones delivering the takeout. They are delivering packages, stocking shelves, ringing up groceries, cleaning subway cars— essential employees forced to keep going to work with a cough and fever until they can't breathe. Or they've lost their jobs as waiters, bartenders, barbers, caregivers, and now they aren't sure how much longer they'll be able to afford a home—an apartment, a basement, a bunk bed—to stay in. Elmhurst is 71 percent foreign-born and over 93 percent people of color. Even before COVID-19, most of its residents were struggling to keep up with the rising cost of shelter. And its population density is particularly lethal in a pandemic: Elmhurst has some of the highest numbers of people per room in the city. There is no way to self-isolate when you are sharing your bedroom and the air you breathe with two or three other people.

A few weeks ago, when I began to feel what was coming for my neighborhood and the world, my body began to rebel. I couldn't eat. My throat closed when I tried to swallow. The next day, while I was lighting a candle to pray, I abruptly shat my pants. I assumed I was becoming an embodied metaphor or cliché, literally shitting myself from sheer fear. But my sister, seriously sick with presumed COVID-19 in Oregon, told me that these were classic presenting symptoms. I called the NYC helpline for advice and the matter-of-fact doctor who spoke to me told me to self-quarantine. I was sick in bed for almost two weeks—chilled, exhausted, parched—and then my symptoms calmed. I still don't know if it was COVID-19 or terror.

I am one of the lucky ones. I'm a professor who lives alone and I can teach and write from home. I'm still being paid. But in a crisis like this, my ongoing distance from friends, family, and the people around me feels intolerable. Before the virus arrived, I used to walk down Broadway or Roosevelt Avenue every day, the 7 train roaring above me, surrounded by the sounds of people speaking to one another in Spanish, Mandarin, Bengali, Nepali, and other languages I couldn't begin to guess, exhilarated by being one body among tens of thousands. Now, after almost a month of total self-isolation, I open my window to the sirens as a way of feeling closer to all the neighbors I can no longer hear or see—many of whom are bearing the brunt of this pandemic.

My neighbors are not the only people I'm yearning to be closer to. In Washington State, my father begins his second month of self-isolation. He has a preexisting lung condition. Just a few miles away from him, my grandmother, who lives in the same town as many of her children, grandchildren, and great-grandchildren, celebrates her ninety-fourth birthday alone. My sense of personal and general dread keeps expanding exponentially.

When will I see my family again? becomes *Will I see my family again?*

When will I touch someone again? becomes *Will I touch someone again?*

When will I chat with my landlady Lily again, and when will I buy a steamed vegetable bun for lunch at Fay Da Bakery, and when will I walk to Northern Boulevard in the golden hour and get a drink at the Queensboro and marvel at the Manhattan skyline glowing like the Celestial City? becomes *Will our whole shared beloved world be reduced to emotional and economic rubble?*

The sirens connect my individual sorrow to our common grief. I've been finding other sounds to connect me to mutual consolation. The night we lost our priest, Father Antonio Checo, my neighbors Gabriel, Pathapong, Katie, and I read psalms and prayed prayers together over the phone. We sang "Amazing Grace." In the midst of death, forbidden the comfort of touch and the grace of one another's physical presence, sound becomes our daily lifeline, our hope to hold, our last intimacy.

The pandemic has turned up the volume on so much preexisting clamor—the grinding gears of exploitation and government lies—but we are countering these sounds of alarm with the sounds of community. With my friends Candice and Sandy, who are home alone in Manhattan and the Bronx, I call members of Congress about rent relief and decarceration, cheer for essential workers each night at 7, and read stories to nephews, nieces, and neighbor kids on FaceTime. We've been making and sending each other scraps of sound throughout the day: true confessions, affirmations, freestyle rhymes, a jazz piano version of "Ain't Misbehavin'." I listen, on constant repeat, to the song they collaborated on last week, "Hug Me through the Phone," gloriously sung by Sandy to an old Motown background track she found on YouTube:

> Will you
> Hug me through the phone
> Don't wanna feel alone
> Hug me through the phone
> I need to feel your glow
> One day we will all be free
> We'll break down walls
> Fight all disease
> We'll stop the wars that
> Make them rich
> Our love
> will always
> be

Never since I was born have I spent more than a day or two without the presence of another person. Now, in my solitude (and its attendant, barely suppressed grief and fear), I've fallen into an unexpected "isolationship" with a Facebook friend I've never met—someone I'd never spoken to before the pandemic. Each night we put our phones next to our pillows, turn on the speakers, and leave them on till morning. The sound of my friend's speech slowly fades into the sound of their breathing. I shut my eyes and listen to their embodied presence: it's the most socially close I am able to be. I am summoning presence through timbre, through our shared and scared laughter, through the sound of steady currents of warm air leaving their lungs. I can almost feel it on my face.

When the sirens blaring through my dreams wake me, I think of the long-ago church bells that used to toll death knells: one toll for each year in the life of the departed. I imagine hundreds of villagers at work in kitchens or fields stopping to listen as they count the years, guessing and grieving the one who has gone. Now all the sounds blur together. Each of the hundreds of overlapping, shrieking, keening wails represents a life, and, perhaps soon, the sounds of mourning that life.

In their intensity, though, the sirens also give voice to the full-throttled anger that comes from knowing that the devastation was preventable, and that it is falling hardest on the people who are least equipped to bear it.

The White String

Brandon Shimoda

One night a few years ago my partner and I went to Wat Buddhametta, a Theravada Buddhist temple in Tucson, Arizona. We had lived in Tucson from 2011 to 2014, moved around for two years, and had just returned. We were exhausted from traveling and were seeking a place, a community, in which to meditate. Our first visit was on chanting night. When we entered, the monk, Ajahn Sarayut Arnanta, was leading a group in chanting the Pāli scriptures. He sat on a platform surrounded by tall vases overflowing with flowers, in front of a golden Buddha. Several white strings (*sai sin* in Thai) looped around the golden Buddha; at least two were connected to Ajahn Sarayut's wrists, and one shot out like spider silk over his head and onto a wooden grid suspended from the ceiling. It passed through the grid, where it seemed to multiply, sending many white strings hanging down to the floor. Fifteen or so people sat beneath the grid, all of them with a piece of string coiled or wrapped around their head, like the frosting on cinnamon buns. Everyone was connected—to the golden Buddha, to Ajahn Sarayut, to each other.

The chanting intensified and deepened the beauty of the grid of string: the rhythmic, droning, cicada-like sound of each voice—of the voices together—transformed the white string from something utilitarian and mundane into a hypha-like network of extrasensory communication.

I had forgotten about the string. But I am describing all this because I had a dream shortly after entering into self-quarantine with my partner and our one-and-a-half-year-old daughter.

The dream—was it two weeks ago, a few days ago?—was simple. It was raining, a downpour. But I saw places in the storm where it was not raining, as if there were columns of air immune to getting wet. And then, in the middle of the rain and the columns of air, amid all the sound, Wat Buddhametta and the grid of white string appeared. In a flash, the golden Buddha was there, and the white string was looped around the golden Buddha, but neither Ajahn Sarayut nor anyone else was there. As before, the white string ran through the wooden grid, and many white strings hung down to the floor.

The fact that the people had been removed from the room was disconcerting not only to me, but also, it seemed in the dream, to the white string. When we had attended chanting night at Wat Buddhametta, I'd paid more attention to the white string than to the people, but now, in my dream, I missed them. I felt that something horrible had happened to them, something beyond mere absence: something more violent. They had been disappeared. But I felt that some part of their voices—some resonance or recollection of pure thinking—existed in the white string. And with that, the flash burned out, and it was raining, and not raining, again.

Today is Monday, March 30. My partner and our daughter and I have been at home for seventeen days. We used to go to the park, five minutes away, with wide-open fields of green grass and trees, so our daughter could run around. Now we take walks around the neighborhood. It is spring in Tucson, trees are leafing out, flowers are in bloom.

> to ward off adversity
> time speeds up the appearance
> of flowers   the children
> play

That is from Etel Adnan's *Time,* translated from the French by the poet Sarah Riggs, which I am currently rereading. "More flowers," my daughter says, walking through flowers.

A menacing silence has fallen upon the world. I imagine that the silence, and its menace, is much louder—maybe even extremely loud—in places that are not the desert, that are far from, or inversions of, the desert. As we walk through the neighborhood young people, old people, people on bicycles, and people with dogs appear but disappear just as quickly, as if they had slipped through a seam in the general mirage of sociality in the age of COVID-19. Actually, it feels more as if the *people* are the mirage, including my family and myself, and the world—the wide and languid streets of Tucson—is the empty room beneath the grid of white string, which still, in our absence, connects us all, maybe even more intensely. Adnan again:

> people come back in our
> dreams to bring us their truth
> that which our eyes refused
> to see, and for which they
> burned us, in burning themselves

I trust my dreams. I trust them especially when I do not trust myself to process what is happening outside them. Is that what I am trying to do now, by remembering, for myself and with you, my dream, and the suddenly delirious and uncertain days and nights before it? Dreams have perfect timing. What originally appeared as a functional, if beautiful, part of daily life, returns, years later, transformed into the legend for—a key to—life in general. The white string is powerful because it is precarious. If someone were to pull too hard on any one piece of the string, the whole thing would come down.

DAYS LATER we returned from another walk around the neighborhood. The flowers were more plentiful and brighter, and more fragrant and effusive, therefore more defiant and mocking. And walking through them were people—young people, old people, people on bicycles, people with dogs—all keeping their distance. And yet there was something beatific about the faces, above the flowers, of people who had spent their day indoors, oscillating between depression and resignation, awareness and forgetting, and the simple agenda of trying to get on.

What is a ghost? A soul that is desperate to return to that which no longer exists? Or the soullessness that has enforced the increasing lack of existence?

We passed a small house with a rusted metal fence. Cut into the vertical slats was a sculpture: six faceless steel figures on a platform. They were like the figures in Giacometti's *Piazza*—walking, yet aimless—but instead of being tall and slender, they were short and squat, as if Giacometti's figures had been hammered, by time and circumstance, deep into themselves. We knew the house, had passed it many times, but had never until tonight noticed the sculpture. "Look!" we said to our daughter. "It's a sculpture!" To which our daughter said, "Sculpture, sculpture, sculpture," and then, as we were walking away, "Sculpture, sculpture, sculpture."

Farther along, as we walked through a stretch of bright yellow and orange daisies, our daughter (her name is Yumi) bent over to smell them, as she does with all flowers, and declared, simply: "Too many."

MAY

Trading Riffs to Slay Monsters

Yusef Komunyakaa and Laren McClung

I know patterns of lockdown & migration—
how a storm or germ could drive us
into a cellar or march us out toward fertile soil.

How a bat in the market can transform
the shape of the future or cause us
to take three steps back & cover our faces

with masks I dreamt in a dream.
Yes, I know we were taught to believe
our machines could control meat & sugar.

I am sorry, but I don't wish to rush
to the fire in the heart of the thing,
drama, or deed. I'm ready to leave

the 1890s, & find myself at the door
of Ed's Museum. But it is closed
because of a slow lockdown in America,

& we're governed by wishful thinking,
voodoo economics, & bankruptcy
while talking about alphabet soup.

You'll find a garden mouse with flowers,
& a pig buried in a pot of dirt
at the step, but that's nothing

like the collection of everyday things
piled up in the heart & mind.
I was just thinking how one man's

treasures show the shortcomings
of a lifetime of people hoarding
iconic junk—false gods & playthings.

For years I'd see this guy pushing
two shopping carts along the city
streets. He'd take one up the block—

walk back & grab the other one—
both piled high with busted clocks,
broken gadgets, bottles, & toys.

Sometimes the poor work hard
pushing a round stone uphill,
the first to die of COVID-19.

I'd say take a deep breath, but
we all know there's no fresh air
at a time like this. My heart breaks

in the middle of the night, when I'm up
arranging letters to leave behind
in the event things don't go as planned.

I know it matters little what we leave,
but since my circadian rhythms
are off, I must busy my hands.

I worked wintertime with Father H
(forbidden to come within a half mile
of Fort Carson & the Air Force

Academy) & those other volunteers
at the soup kitchen where we'd serve
food plucked from Safeway dumpsters

at midnight, before they poured bleach
on the day-old bread & unspoiled fruit
& vegetables under godly moonlight.

Look, my great-uncle wore a heavy coat
in late August & wandered avenues
or rocked himself to sleep on city benches.

Sometimes a knock at the door meant
he hadn't eaten for days. He carried
a duffel bag with a change of clothes

& his drumsticks & he'd beat triplets
on a bucket in the yard. Did he first
know hunger in the year he marched?

Leaving Yale for the Coronavirus Epicenter

Eric O'Keefe-Krebs

Mom is asthmatic, so I go into CVS alone. It's 7 in the morning. We came early to avoid a crowd. Toilet paper, paper towels, trash bags—in and out. I hold my breath through the automatic doors, past the line, down the aisle.

The place looks as it always has, but it's scary now. Old scenery doesn't match the new dread. Apocalyptic scenery would help—rivers of bile, swarms of locusts, something biblical, something as other-worldly as this all feels. Instead, you're afraid against familiar back-drops—afraid at the supermarket, afraid at the pharmacy, afraid in your own home. The nearest hospital is Elmhurst Hospital—where, on March 26, thirteen deaths in a day signaled to the city that things were about to get far worse. Today there are so many corpses that they are kept cold in tractor trailers parked on the street outside.

Ten minutes and five fumbled credit card swipes later, I make it back to the car and sanitize furiously. The safety perimeter my family has constructed with hand soap and raw ginger diminishes with each day. A friend's grandfather first. My cousins' aunt second. An electrician my dad did his apprenticeship with third.

"When I pray, I always start with the whole world," Mom tells me as we drive back, "and then I narrow it to my family—so God doesn't think I'm selfish."

I have class in an hour, and Mom has work. We strip the groceries of their packaging, wipe down fruits. There's nowhere to go, nothing to do but reduce risk of infiltration. Nothing gets in, nothing gets out. Dad's already out in a manhole somewhere keeping the internet on. Last week he got a letter asking for his continued support as an essential worker. So on nights when I stay up too late—the nocturnal college student is a hard part to stop playing—I hear his alarm through the wall. He slouches down the hall, to the bathroom, the kitchen, twenty minutes of TV news, and out the door.

Drive around the city with him and he'll point out every building he's wired, every bridge he's climbed, every manhole he's descended into. He has never felt safer at work, he tells us at dinner to calm our nerves. "No cars on the road."

We've been flipping through old family photo albums after we eat. It's the first time in forever all five of us—Mom, Dad, my two older sisters, and myself—have consistently shared a meal, with matching plates and silverware set orderly on the table and literally nowhere else for anyone to be. Except Dad. Dad still has to go to work.

Middle Village, Queens, is a geriatric and innately morbid neighborhood, boxed in on three sides by cemeteries. In the mid-nineteenth century, when property values in Manhattan rose, hundreds of thousands of bodies were exhumed from city cemeteries and shipped to the Brooklyn-Queens border. Even our park, which used to be a swamp, has a few headstones in it. Transplants and gentrifiers like to talk about the city as a collection of atomized, interchangeable commuters, always moving on to the next thing, the next address. But my neighborhood's most notable trait is how infrequently people leave. Most of our neighbors' families have lived here for two or three generations, mine included. Dad grew up four blocks from where we live now; of his three siblings, he moved the farthest.

Tonight's photo album: "Home Improvements, 1991," from when

Mom and Dad first moved into the house we've lived in ever since. My family is one of tradespeople, people who work with calloused hands and make things. Carpenters, bricklayers, electricians, plumbers, mechanics, ironworkers. As one of the first to go to college, I balance the desire to earn enough money to hire contractors and the desire to be skilled enough that I'll never have to.

In the photos, I see my family as they were thirty years ago: Aunt Donna scrubbing the corners of the bathroom; Aunt Ginger leaning on a paint-stained stepladder; Uncle Dennis poking his head out from the hole where a sink once was. Peering down from what would become my bedroom, Mom captures Papa, trowel in hand, kneeling over a freshly poured driveway. The driveway leads to the backyard that for twenty-two years we shared with Dolly, the neighbor who became a second mother to my mom soon after my parents moved in, then a second grandmother to all of us kids. I used to stand on the toilet and talk to her across the driveway. My bedroom window looked into her kitchen. She's gone now, taken by the coronavirus last week.

Today I'm back in the baby-blue room my crib was in: where I peed the bed; where I had bad dreams; where my mom lay next to me all night when I was too nervous to sleep before the first day of school; where I developed my internet addiction on a secondhand laptop; where I lamented crushes; where I waded through endless piles of homework, studied for the SAT, worried over acceptance rates at the colleges I wanted to attend, and packed my bags when it all paid off.

Now the room I devoted my life to getting out of is where I go to college. In the digital lecture hall, I see the other students, mostly at home like me. Surrounded by baby blue or lilac, their fellowships canceled, their moms passing by in the background, their internships denied, their dog interrupting—their short-term, mid-term, and long-term plans upended. Movers and shakers, all stagnant for the time being.

On the stairs my sisters weep. The assistant principal of their old high school—a forty-two-year-old man, the heart and soul of their all-girls Catholic school—died of the virus, leaving three kids and a wife behind. The local news reported on the death, a thirty-second memorial with clips from students and faculty who knew him. Nothing about Middle Village was ever news before, aside from the occasional downed power line.

In the kitchen Mom leans on Dad's chest. "You can't go back to work."

Now Dad goes to work wearing a mask.

It's not the first time he's done so. A few days after 9/11, he was working near Ground Zero as part of the recovery efforts. He was told that the air was clear, that it was safe to breathe. Dad didn't believe it. He wore a mask. Every year he gets a physical to keep an eye on whether the toxins that have taken the lives of over two thousand first and second responders have caught up to him. So far, so good.

Fancy schools like Yale, for those like myself from blue-collar backgrounds, are means of getting out. They offer pedigree and knowledge and a spot on the corporate board of your choosing. They're places meant to carry you away from your small bedroom, from the eternally-on TV, from arguments over money, from your neighborhood nickname and the people who still use it. The virus has forced students like me back home, with nothing more than school-wide half-baked emails full of aphorisms about the immateriality of community connecting us to our brief stint in the ivory tower.

But that community, focused so much on personal achievement and enrichment, feels small right now. The lonely climb up the class precipice tricks you into thinking that all ascension occurs in spite of where you began, not because of it. Staring through the mosaic of webcams during class, I don't think about the lecture hall we should all be in or the future my fellow Yale students and I were forging together. I see what my classmates have to lose, too—their pasts that could disappear.

Two months ago I feared that the virus would take me back to Middle Village—to the world of working-class familial obligation I sought to escape. Now, newly thankful for what I've run from, I'm wondering what I was striving for. My community is people who make things. People who make errands into a communal affair. People who glean hours of coffee-and-Entenmann's-fueled laughter from nothing. People who *always* show up, usually unannounced. People who render walls invisible and distance meaningless, a patchwork quilt of family and near-family who embody everything "relatedness" means. People content with going nowhere, and doing it together.

Then I was full of aspirations. Now I fear the virus will take Middle Village from me, that I'll be reduced to remembering it before I ever got the chance to leave.

Welcome to Zoom University

Sean Lynch

Moments of catastrophe possess a terrifying clarity. When systems fail, illusions fall away, bringing to light buried and often unsettling truths. The COVID-19 pandemic and our government's failure to respond to it adequately have exposed many such truths about the systems that structure our daily existence. When the lieutenant governor of Texas suggested that senior citizens would give up their lives for the sake of the economy, he said aloud what many have long intuited: our economic system cares about human beings only insofar as they are human capital. And so catastrophe illuminates what the everyday blurs.

Higher education might not be the most obvious place to witness the terrifying clarity of COVID-19. The structural failures of our health care system have been much more evident and lethal. But for me and millions of other students, faculty, and administrators, the pandemic's disruption of university life has been a revelation. Now that Harvard and Yale (where I am a senior) are forced to adopt the same virtual education models as for-profit universities such as the University of Phoenix, the future of higher education that many have been predicting for years has suddenly arrived.

For the past two centuries, the history of higher education in America has largely been the history of the liberal university. Recognizing the link between education and a democratic society, American intellectuals as far back as Emerson put forward a distinctive vision of the university. Rather than simply indoctrinating students in a tradition or training them for a specific career, the university should expose them to new ideas and teach them to think for themselves. While today we mostly associate liberal education with elite private institutions, this ideal also informed the establishment of great public universities. Teaching literature and mathematics as well as agriculture and engineering, public universities aimed to make a liberal education widely accessible. Although this aim often foundered on preexisting social hierarchies, it also anticipated and galvanized changes in those hierarchies. In my home state of Nebraska, for instance, the state university provided for the education of female students in its 1869 charter—a hundred years before Yale admitted its first female undergraduate.

Given the influence of public universities on American life, the liberal idea of higher education has come to shape how many of us think and feel about the university. Like many young Americans, I saw college as more than a next step after high school. The university possessed a special glamour, and as I grew older, I identified this glamour with the infinite freedom to redefine myself—with the project of self-discovery. Influenced by the aesthetic of countless books and films, I envisioned grassy quads, autumn leaves, and wood-paneled seminar rooms. I longed for conversations that would run late into the night and the bustle of portrait-lined dining halls. And while it is true that the reality of college has tempered my idealization, more remarkable is the degree to which it has preserved it, at least until now.

But American universities are rapidly moving away from their underlying ethos. Facing budget cuts, many public and smaller private universities have begun to transform themselves into services. In exchange for luxurious living spaces and professional development, these universities are demanding that students pay increasingly exorbitant tuitions. Universities have also started to evaluate academic affairs in light of profitability. In 2018, for example, the University of Nebraska proposed cutting its art history and geography departments even as it was preparing to announce a $155 million stadium expansion for its revenue-generating football team. These shifts in the priorities of higher education have made even public universities increasingly unaffordable and have opened the door for online institutions like the University of Phoenix or remote-learning platforms like Coursera. Highlighting their relative affordability and flexibility, these companies claim that virtual learning represents the future of higher education. And they have data to back them up. According to the National Center for Education Statistics, 33 percent of university students in 2018 were enrolled in at least one "distance education course," and 15 percent of all students were enrolled exclusively in such courses. For a growing number of students at private and public universities alike, the experience of going to college may soon consist of opening a laptop.

The COVID-19 pandemic has made this possible future a present reality. Like millions of other students, I now go to class by clicking on a Zoom link, which transforms me into one of a dozen pixelated heads. Having a good internet connection and a quiet space, I'm able to follow along better than I had expected. But the experience of learning in this way is nonetheless isolating. Classroom conversations that would once have continued in the hallway or dining hall now end with the decision to "leave the meeting" and the abrupt disappearance of classmates' faces from the screen. One moment I'm discussing Wallace Stevens; the next I'm staring at a blank wall, alone.

The isolation of online learning is just one of the many ways that classes this semester are undermining the liberal ethos. The very idea of the university as a place where students learn to collaborate and think for themselves feels absurd when we are going to school in our parents' basements. Moreover, unequal access to resources like reliable internet connections and quiet study spaces belies the principle of equality inherent in that ideal. Whereas I can get away from my family to read Stevens, other students are forced to look after younger siblings or help out with struggling family businesses. Pandemics may affect everyone, but they do not affect everyone equally. Outside the comparatively egalitarian spaces of the university, the disparities between students' lives grow stark.

But of course liberal education is not merely an ethos, it is also an aesthetic, and one that many universities are fighting hard to preserve. Yale, for instance, recently released custom Zoom backgrounds featuring various views of campus and, like many universities, is planning for a virtual commencement. But for all their good intentions, these efforts to ensure continuity often appear rather ridiculous. Images of campus cannot replace the feeling of being on campus. A virtual commencement cannot provide the sense of community and celebration that an actual one conveys. And so one cannot help wondering whether the emptiness of these efforts reveals another unsettling truth. Is the aesthetic of the university a representation of its underlying ethos, or is it a screen for concealing its steady erosion? If universities continue to move away from the ideals of liberal education, the way we feel about the university, as well as the rituals we associate with it, will have to change. The losses of this semester thus stand as portents of all that we risk losing permanently.

The COVID-19 pandemic will eventually abate, and at some point afterward a new class of students will arrive on college campuses, full of aspirations for the next four years. But as they try to reinvent themselves with the help of their classes, professors, and peers, they will be confronting an education system that is itself in the process of reinvention. The social and economic forces driving the university's abandonment of liberal education predate COVID-19 and will outlast it. Still, perhaps the terrifying clarity that the pandemic has brought to bear on preexisting changes to the purpose of the university offers us a chance to resist them. The future of liberal education may look grim, but we can reclaim it by demanding greater funding for public universities from state governments and a shift in funding priorities from university administrators. Our choice to demand these changes now will ensure that the isolation and inequality of higher education this semester remain temporary. This moment of catastrophe, put simply, is the time to act.

Reading *The Decameron* through the Lens of COVID-19

Millicent Marcus

Giovanni Boccaccio's *Decameron* is best known in the English-speaking world as a precursor to Chaucer's *Canterbury Tales.* But of late it's gained an unexpected prominence—and relevance—thanks to the coronavirus pandemic. Written in the immediate aftermath of the Black Death that struck Florence in 1348, the book tells the story of a group of ten young people who flee the plague-ravaged city for the Tuscan countryside, where they bide their time telling one hundred short tales over the course of their pastoral retreat. I've been reading, teaching, and writing about *The Decameron* ever since graduate school. But it had never held up a mirror to my own life experience until now. Indeed, while I had always been able to balance readerly pleasure with the demands of disinterested scholarship when I read Boccaccio, I had kept the book's introductory chronicle of the pandemic at a "safe" critical distance, as a relic of the archival past.

All that changed in March. I was teaching a seminar on *The Decameron* when the coronavirus hit, and the impact of the pandemic forced me to rethink my entire relationship to the text. Whereas the plague had once seemed like a remote historical event, far from the medically advanced and technologically sophisticated reaches of today's world, it now became frighteningly real. Rereading the book in the light of what was happening all around me, I came to understand that I had been engaging in a practice of "literary distancing," resisting the workings of identification and empathy that bind readers to characters in fictional works.

This kind of distancing can, of course, be useful—and even necessary—for a scholar. But in the case of *The Decameron,* the critical distancing I was engaged in was, I now think, a defensive move, one that cordoned off the physical and social collapse besetting Boccaccio's characters. My detachment from the sufferings of the people of Florence suddenly seemed like smugness and complacency.

Although the Black Death was much more deadly than the coronavirus has so far been, I began to see uncanny parallels between our time and Boccaccio's—rhetorical and thematic emphases in our time that contain unmistakable echoes of Boccaccio's work. When in April Governor Andrew Cuomo compared his mitigation measures to a difficult ascent, to be followed by the arrival in a beautiful place on the "other side of the mountain," I could not help thinking of Boccaccio's assurance that his frame story's climb up a "steep and rugged mountain" would lead to a "beautiful and delightful plain." In a similar vein, just as Boccaccio described the grisly spectacle of cadavers awaiting collection (family members "carried the bodies of the recently deceased out of their houses and put them down by the door fronts"), so the *New York Times* reported on April 9, "Normally, workers from the city's Office of Chief Medical Examiner arrive within a few hours to collect a body. Now the wait can be as long as 24 hours." Even Boccaccio's grim account of the lax observance of funeral rites and burial practices has found its contemporary analogue in stories of people unable to be at their relatives' bedside to hear their final words.

In *The Decameron,* the breakdown of mourning rites is but one example of the generalized social collapse that beset the disease-ridden city. "In the midst of so much affliction and misery," Boccaccio wrote, "respect for the reverend authority of the laws, both divine and human, had declined just about to the vanishing point." The coronavirus may not have wreaked similar havoc on our communities, yet Boccaccio's description of the way "citizens avoided one another . . . almost no one took care of his neighbors, and . . . relatives visited one another infrequently" captures something important about the way most of us have been forced to live. Boccaccio described people using one of three adaptive modes—modes many of us may recognize—to deal with the virus: lockdown into isolated communities, well-stocked with "delicate foods and the best wines" to be consumed in moderation; untrammeled pursuit of pleasure—heavy drinking, merrymaking, and promiscuous consorting with fellow revelers; and a middle course, "neither restricting their diet so much as the first, nor letting themselves go in drinking and other forms of dissipation so much as the second, but doing just enough to satisfy their appetites."

The definitive blow to my "literary distancing" impulse came not from today's journalistic echoes of Boccaccio's account but from my students' personal reactions to reading *The Decameron* in the time of COVID-19. Once we resumed our seminars via Zoom, the pain my students were feeling at being isolated from the campus community and their yearning for connection and solidarity became clear. This made me see *The Decameron*'s frame story—ten young aristocrats (members of Boccaccio's *brigata,* party of friends) amusing themselves by telling stories as they hid from the plague—in a whole new light.

I had always felt alienated from these characters, who display the most elegant manners and enjoy the luxurious ease of their pastoral retreat with an army of servants in tow. So that no practical matters would impinge on the young people's leisure, each brigata member is asked to donate his or her own personal servant to oversee some particular aspect of the group's material needs. With the assignment of those tasks complete, the brigata members are free to engage in the activities for which they are best suited—entertaining one another through song and dance (music courtesy of Dioneo on the lute and Fiammetta on the viol), game playing (backgammon and chess), pleasant conversation, strolls along garden and woodland paths, and storytelling.

In my previous reading, I had historicized these young people's behaviors, seeing them as emblems of medieval social-class stratification, and I considered their need for storytelling as yet one more example of their escapist desires. But listening to my students as they dealt with the loss of the community that had bound their lives together on campus, I came to think about the brigata's role within the overall plan of *The Decameron* differently. It now seems to me that the young storytellers' deep communal ties and the rigorous order of their routines—governed by a rotating monarchy they set up to preside over their daily activities—serve a vital function, forming a fire wall against the social ruin brought on by the plague. It's especially telling that Boccaccio ushered the brigata members onto *The Decameron* stage by highlighting their interpersonal bonds—friendship, neighborliness, kinship, and romantic love—affirming the very social ties that had been undone by the ravages of the plague. And the reason they devote so much time to spinning tales is because this, more than other activities, promotes group concord, as Pampinea explains: "We should not spend the hot part of the day playing games, for they necessarily leave one of the players feeling miffed, without giving that much pleasure either to his opponent or to those who are watching. Rather, we should tell stories, for even though just one person is doing the talking, all the others will still have the pleasure of listening."

In this mild affirmation of the social harmony that her storytelling promotes, Pampinea understates the cultural significance of what the brigata is doing. Far from a way of merely whiling away the time in a sedentary activity that wouldn't involve competition, this epic weaving of one hundred tales, set in locations throughout the Mediterranean world, spanning eras from classical and biblical times to the present, embracing the humblest and the loftiest of characters, and including every genre available within the repertory of medieval fiction making—can be seen as a feat of heroism in its own right: a rescue operation for a civilization under threat of collapse.

There may be something self-congratulatory in this reading, of course, given my own privileged position as a professor at an elite university, finding refuge from the present-day scourge by reading and analyzing the brigata's stories with my intellectually gifted seminar students. Even so, in this case the impulse to forgo literary distancing—in the era of *social* distancing—has been critically fruitful, enabling me to acknowledge our shared human vulnerability to natural disaster across time. In the process, I have learned to set aside my distaste for the aristocratic airs of the brigata members in favor of a deep appreciation for the strength of the communal bonds that enabled them to survive, and for the power embedded in the simple act of telling a story.

A Commencement Deferred

Meghana Mysore

My *thatha* (grandfather) is sitting on the terrace of his apartment in Bangalore, India. It is morning there and nighttime here in Portland, Oregon, where I'm living with my parents. It's more than seven weeks into India's nationwide lockdown, ten weeks since my university announced that students had to depart campus. In Bangalore, no one can leave the house except to pick up essential groceries and medicine. Thatha left his apartment once only, to get pills for a sudden outbreak of shingles. He misses the walks he used to take through the park with his four close friends, when they would exchange snippets from their favorite poems.

On the phone, Thatha is silent for a while, his breathing labored. "What do you see outside?" I ask him. "Ghostly, empty streets," he says. "Police officers standing at each corner." He asks me what I see. I'm sitting at the desk in my childhood bedroom, where I made my way through elementary, middle, and high school, the bookshelf filled with picture books and novels by Patricia Polacco and Enid Blyton.

I think about how I was supposed to be receiving my diploma on campus at Yale University this Monday, and for a moment I ache for the memories that will not be made. To distract myself, I ask Thatha about my mother's undergraduate years at Lady Shri Ram College, a women's liberal arts school, in New Delhi. He pauses, then laughs, recalling the time she came home late from school with a scarf wrapped conspicuously around her head, afraid that her grandfather would not approve of her short haircut. I laugh, too. Our merriment carries into our separate air, and for a moment we are together in the space of the past.

AS GRADUATION APPROACHES, my life has been filled with congratulatory video calls, but my mind is stuck on the final day before spring break, when my suitemates and I had dinner at Mecha Noodle on Crown Street in New Haven. We took a photo before we ate, our heads curving together over bowls of soup. It was the last time we saw one another.

One afternoon near the semester's end, I am sitting with my mother at our dining table, steam wafting from our cups of Earl Grey. She takes out an old photo album, stops at a picture of her and her lecturers at Lady Shri Ram College, all clad in bright orange, blue, pink, or red saris. This was April 1988, the final day of classes. My mother explains to me that there wasn't a festive celebration; she and her classmates simply gathered in the canteen with their lecturers to reminisce. My mother stands at the back left, looking down at the ground. "Without this picture," she says softly, touching the photo's edges, "I wouldn't have a memory of the day I graduated."

As is conventional for college students in India, my mother lived at home during her four years at Lady Shri Ram, her days following a predictable routine. She and a tight group of girlfriends would do "simple things," like visit Connaught Place, a market teeming with stalls selling scarves and jewelry, or drink chai at one another's houses. "We sat in classrooms together, we went to the canteen and talked."

She flips back in the photo album to a picture of herself and her girlfriends on a college outing to Tilyar Lake. Separated over the years by time and distance, my mother and her Lady Shri Ram friends have struggled to stay in contact. "Looking at these pictures," she tells me, "it's almost like I'm traveling back in time."

At twenty-two, as she neared the end of her master's program at Delhi University, my mother became engaged through an arranged marriage to my father. "I was going into something I didn't know. I didn't know what the next day would hold." She was afraid of not fitting in with my father's family and their way of life. "I gave up everything I knew."

In early 1990, soon after marrying, my parents emigrated from Bangalore to Sydney, Australia, wanting to see if they could make it on their own. As my mother describes it, she and my father, utterly unfamiliar with the city or the culture, faced the added challenge of finding themselves in a country experiencing a deep recession. "I felt uprooted," she says, lifting out a photo of herself in front of security at Sydney Airport. In it, she stares blankly ahead, unsmiling. "It took me a long time to adjust. I'd never lived away from my parents. I started missing Indian food. I didn't know where to get Indian groceries."

In the past two months, I've felt suspended—physically stuck at home, unable to move forward from my time at Yale. The days are repetitive, but time pulses forward. On Monday, May 18, at 8 a.m., bleary-eyed, I will wake, listen to President Salovey's address, and officially graduate from Yale. Though the past week has been crowded with events to remind seniors that we are indeed graduating, it is difficult to process this reality, because the chapter of my life feels unfinished. Despite the language about new beginnings, most of us are "moving on" but not moving.

In her essay "To Speak Is to Blunder," Yiyun Li writes, "One crosses the border to become a new person. One finishes a manuscript and cuts off the characters. One adopts a language. These are false and forced frameworks, providing illusory freedom." At my age my mother moved from one country to another, but she felt stuck upon arrival. "Those first few months in Australia, I was always thinking of the next time I could travel to Delhi and see my parents," she says. Those months were so painful that she has never been able to talk about them. I notice she recounts her memories in English, not Kannada, and I wonder if using her second language offers her a kind of distance. She speaks in a calm and considered voice, as though she is talking about another person, a self whose experiences are not quite her own.

After giving birth to my sister in Sydney—a year before she and my father moved to the United States, where I was born—my mother finally started feeling at home in her new life. She bought a *chabudai* (a Japanese dining table) at a local market, and though she didn't know how to use it, she found its soft purple color inexplicably comforting. She started walking around the city every day with a group of other pregnant women, who became her friends. On weekends she took the train to neighboring suburbs, and one day she signed up for a typing class at a local vocational school. She remembers the tea and biscuits that always sat on the counter in the school kitchen and the gentle voice of her teacher, Fay. "I thought I'd forgotten all this," she says to me now, her face brightening as though she is hearing her own stories for the first time.

When I first moved back home in March, I spoke with a concerned professor over the phone, telling him that I was having trouble making meaning of everything that was happening. "You need distance to make meaning," he said. "You need time." I wonder if it is time that has shaped the chaos of my mother's past into a story she is finally able to share with me.

I am afraid of what I will forget. I am afraid that I will lose touch with my closest friends as we've been pushed prematurely apart. We seem different from who we were on campus—and also distant from who we used to be when we lived at home.

I imagine my mother at twenty-two, arriving at Sydney Airport, staring at the stranger snapping her photo, unsure and afraid. I imagine her walking with a group of pregnant women in Sydney, women she has not kept in touch with but who nonetheless gave her a sense of solidarity in this transitional period of her life. I think of the small, repetitive actions that have pulled me through the last two months—walking with my high school friend, driving around the block and waving from the window at my neighbors—and how unexpected people and places have become the tapestry of my final moments "in" college.

AS IMMIGRANTS, my parents are acquainted with the U.S. educational system only through my sister and me. Seeing me graduate from an American university today would have been a triumph for them. When they came to this country, my parents shared the hope that so many immigrants have for their children: that we would face fewer uncertainties than they had. For them, college graduation is the ultimate materialization of their efforts, a ceremonial confirmation that their difficult choice has paid off. That feeling of culmination deferred, they too are facing an array of emotions, struggling to find a sense of closure for themselves.

Late at night after talking with my grandfather in Bangalore about his life in lockdown, I tiptoe downstairs to the living room. My mother and father are fast asleep. I pull the photo album from the shelf below the TV and flip to the picture of my mother in Sydney Airport. I take it out of its slot. I begin to see the arc of my mother's life—a confusing transition that ultimately leads to this house where she raised two daughters and grew to middle age with a man who was once a stranger to her—and I begin to imagine the potential arc of mine. One day, far in the future, I may be telling my own daughter about this time: how, as a second-semester senior in college, I used to meander my childhood neighborhood's streets for hours, lonely and restless; how I finished my college thesis in my childhood bedroom; how I graduated from my laptop screen. "Rarely does a story start where we wish it had, or end where we wish it would," Li writes. But somewhere in all the chaos is a story, if we are given the time to see it.

History Is Another Word for Trauma

Rachel Jamison Webster

One Wednesday last month, I learned that my aunt Cynthia was dying of coronavirus. She had declined to be intubated or put on a ventilator. By the time I knew she had the virus, she had already been sedated and was floating in some liminal place between breath and non-breath.

Cynthia had worked as a laboratory technician and understood what was happening. A week earlier, when my mother had called her to talk about the pandemic, Cynthia had explained the wily, adaptive ways that viruses reproduce. Bacteria replicate in straight lines, but viruses are eccentric survivors, she'd said. They will do anything to perpetuate themselves.

I DIDN'T MEET my aunt Cynthia until I was sixteen. I had decided that I wanted to be a writer and insisted on wearing battered Chuck Taylors and a corduroy hat to all of my college interviews, thinking that this made me look like a beatnik intellectual. I had grown up in rural Ohio. I wrote poems and plays, designed my own clothes, stopped eating meat, read incessantly, and did plein air paintings. My straitlaced family didn't quite know what to do with me. Then one day my mother said, apparently offhandedly, "My aunt Cynthia writes. We should go visit so you can meet her."

Cynthia lived with her partner in a manor house in Surry County, Virginia. They chain-smoked, talked about literature, submitted stories and poems to periodicals, and rented out rooms to boarders. They raised chickens, grew their own produce, and cooked delicious, elaborate meals. There were peacocks roaming around on the lawn. Fresh garden flowers and alabaster lamps in the bedrooms. A few mischievous kittens, an old black rescue dog, and a pickup truck that Cynthia had named the Silver Queen.

My mother and I settled into the big kitchen with the blue-painted cabinets, smoke-stained ceilings, newspapers and books everywhere. It was the first time I had ever seen *Poetry* magazine. Cynthia cracked open a beer, set a bottle of Blue Nun in front of me, and said, "Be your own policeman."

We liked—no, loved—each other immediately, with the kind of affinity that thrums in the blood and announces the soul's recognition. There was nothing obligatory about our relationship. It was a cross-generational friendship founded on the relief of seeing someone and being seen so clearly. After college, I returned to Cynthia's house for a couple of months to soak in her world. We'd read, write, and putter in the garden during the day, then cook and drink in the evenings while Cynthia told me stories.

Cynthia's mother, Hazel, was my great-grandmother and the ancestor who most fascinated me. As a teenager Hazel had gotten pregnant with my grandmother, but then left her in her crib in rural Iowa, so I had heard about Hazel mostly as an absence—the selfish, abandoning mother. But Cynthia had adored her, and she filled in the blanks. Hazel went to New York, where she worked as a model and artist before making her way to London. There she fell in love with an officer in the British Army. She got pregnant again and followed him to India by ship, surprising him with her arrival. They married, and a couple of months later, she gave birth on the way to the hospital in Calcutta.

Cynthia was that baby, cherished by her young, glamorous parents. Hazel wore saris, smoked opium, and got to know the poet Rabindranath Tagore. When World War II began, Hazel and Cynthia went back to London, where they narrowly survived the Blitz. Cynthia remembered sheltering in a coat closet under the stairs while bombs obliterated the opposite side of the building. They left London to return to New York, where Hazel checked Cynthia into an orphanage so she could put herself through nursing school. Cynthia, even then a free spirit, teased the nuns, picked locks, staged plays, and ran a black market of pilfered candy.

As an adult, Cynthia joined the first tour of the Peace Corps and went to Malaysia, then called Malaya. After earning her master's degree in laboratory science, she ran a lab in Norfolk, Virginia. She rode a motorcycle, painted, and wrote. She once seduced a priest, but mostly she slept and lived with women.

Cynthia had arrived in my life exactly when I needed her, when I was afraid I would never escape my conventional upbringing. I was fascinated by her freedom, by the stories she had lived, and by the ways her life intersected with history. I didn't understand then what I've begun to realize since—that living through dramatic stories usually means living through trauma, and that the chapters that qualify as "history," like the coronavirus pandemic, are at once overwhelmingly vast and intimately specific.

IF IT WERE NOT this specific time in history, if she'd had anything but coronavirus, if hospitals were allowing visitations, I would have booked a flight to make it to Cynthia before she died. The only thing that mitigated the crazed, helpless feeling of not being there to hold

Cynthia's hand was the fact that most of our communication had been out of body.

For nearly thirty years, Cynthia sent me weekly or monthly letters that functioned almost like journals for her, full of news of the garden, humorous observations, memories of the war, and stories of past lovers. "Dear Mind of My Mind," she'd begin sometimes, speaking to the closeness of our relationship and to the practice of reflection that was central to her wit and resilience.

Without being didactic, Cynthia's letters showed me how to live. She wrote to me through my twenties, when I was living in Chicago, going to school and working. She wrote to me through my thirties, when I married, and when I left my husband for a musician and moved to Kauai. She wrote when I unexpectedly got pregnant. She wrote when my partner was diagnosed with ALS, and I realized that I would somehow have to support our family financially while caring for him as he gradually grew more paralyzed and died. After we learned his diagnosis, she wrote:

> You must drop the dream, roll up your sleeves, tuck your hair behind your ears, thin your lips, pull your gaze away from the horizon and focus on the unexploded bomb in the garden. This is how war is. And this is how survival is.

And a postscript:

> This was a different kind of letter for me to write you. But I felt I had to. I have had more brutal choices presented to me than I thought I could bear. I BORE. Was I stronger for the experiences? No, never. Just braver, less naïve. There really is a dark side of the moon. There are also sunrises, birdsong, stained glass, hot dogs on the grill . . .

Living, Cynthia understood, didn't only mean forging ahead with exuberance. It also meant loving fully, making impossible decisions, and living on after losing the people we cannot imagine living without. At the same time, it meant taking ownership of your life as a space of perception, pleasure, and meaning. In one letter Cynthia recalled a scene in London with her mother:

> I can still smell the cloth as I stood beside her treadle sewing machine. We had a basement flat in Kensington, and in winter the light was low early in the evening. I had a block of plasticine—four sticks in primary colors. Mama let me roll out my creations on the right side of the machine table. I would idly roll balls, and I remember thinking that I could roll one so big that it would go on forever until it was too big to be imagined. I told my mother, and she said, "Of course. That's called infinity. It's the forever place."

Rereading Cynthia's letters is to sense the forever self, the historical self, and the sensory self mingling on the page. It is to be reminded that these moments of heightened connection can be a stay against the relentless passage of time. Cynthia would often interrupt her memories with descriptions of the present moment:

> God, I wish you could smell the beef, carrots, oils and the hair of wine, snips of thyme and parsley. Bubble and toil, no troubles. It is thickening from flour dredging and trying to lure the potatoes in. I can think of nothing more satisfying than writing while one cooks.

These details weren't fillers. They were her life. In sharing her life with me, she was tenderizing us both to what a life can mean. Survival, she kept showing me, is intimately related to creativity, and enhanced by articulating your particular insights, griefs, and delights. This reflective writing makes the inner life real and the self more individuated while acknowledging that we are always shaped by other people and by the times outside.

I think of what Cynthia survived: World War II, the orphanage, the tragedy of her parents' brilliance, addictions, and deaths, as well as her marginalization as a queer person who was ahead of her time. She lived through several historical epochs with utter élan, and she went out on another one called the coronavirus pandemic. She would not be able to describe this one to me. But she had shown me something about living, and now dying, consciously.

AFTER I HEARD THE NEWS, I stayed up all night rereading Cynthia's letters as a way of sitting vigil. I shivered with a kindred coldness, my shirt soaked with tears. The sun rose, and although it was mid-April, I saw that snow had fallen during the night, blanketing everything in white. It was just the kind of unlikelihood that Cynthia would appreciate. I would have begun a letter with it. I would have told her about the skeletal shapes of the trees and the pink magnolia blossoms bowing under snow like sodden cotton.

Cynthia Erskine died on April 22 of complications from coronavirus.

The Children Know

Emily Ziff Griffin

In 1987, when I was eight years old, the same age my daughter is now, my father—a vibrant, thirty-seven-year-old gay man—was diagnosed with AIDS. He was already sick, though not so sick that he couldn't function. At first I had only hints of what was going on: the carefully organized pill bottles that appeared atop his tall dresser; the anxious conversations among his friends outside the market in Fire Island Pines on weekend mornings; the new dentist because my father's old one would no longer see him.

Then one night, my dad sat me down with an issue of *National Geographic* that detailed the AIDS crisis, and he told me he was ill. "Most people who contract AIDS do die," he said. Yet he tried to instill a sense of optimism in my very young mind, showing me a photo of the virus and telling me that the receptors inside his cells could be "blocked" by endorphins—meaning that the more joy he experienced, the fewer pathways the virus would have to infect him.

As an adult I would come to realize that my father's tactic was meant to remind me of the importance of joy even in the face of death; it was, I believe, meant to empower me, to give me a weapon against a disease for which there was no viable treatment. To a child it seemed a vague proposition, with no way to quantify results. I was unsure how to create joy when all I felt was fear and sadness. Even joyful activities became increasingly tarnished by the limitations my father's disease caused. A bike ride in Central Park ended with him unable to keep pace. A trip to Europe was cut short because he was running a fever. Joy, it seemed, was not a cure.

It took five years for my father to succumb to AIDS, his body ultimately ravaged and wasted by Kaposi's sarcoma, which left him unable to walk for months before he finally died. He was hospitalized multiple times with infections, each one bringing the specter of his death ever closer. Each good-bye carried with it the possibility of never seeing each other again. Each hug felt like it had to convey the vastness of our love for what might be the last time. I had my first panic attack in the hospital visiting my dad; he was getting a transfusion and the IV became dislodged from his arm, drenching the bed linens in blood.

During those years, many colleagues and friends of my parents who worked in the arts in New York City also lost their lives. The terror that imbued that time was very real, spurred at first by a lack of information—it took time for people to understand that AIDS was caused by a virus, that the virus was transmitted by the exchange of bodily fluids, that it was initially spreading through unprotected sexual intercourse between men, that it was preventable. Later it was spurred by the fact that AIDS was almost always fatal and, as even I as a child understood, the government didn't seem to care.

The panic and stigma associated with the disease led people to lose their jobs, to be ostracized from their communities, to be feared simply for breathing the same air, occupying the same space. I weathered my father's illness in isolation and in shame. Afraid I would be shunned, I never spoke about it with friends, or even my parents. I stared at the phone in my darkened bedroom at night, afraid it would ring with the news he was gone. I bargained with a god I didn't believe in, begging for a miracle. Knowing that my father was vulnerable to infection, I came to see the world as toxic and dangerous. And my father's eventual death on some level told me: those fears were warranted, and I had failed. I was not able to save him.

With the arrival of COVID-19, I felt agency I didn't have then. A week before it was mandated, I pulled my young kids from their school. Just by walling ourselves off, I told them, we could be saving lives. I reframed this experience around a positive message of care for others. My father's death, I had explained in December, on what would have been their grandfather's seventieth birthday, was rooted in the lack of such care. I revealed then that a strange sickness had appeared and begun killing gay men. I told them our government didn't do enough to stop it. I expressed my outrage over this loss and they mirrored it back—how dare they let Grandpa Charlie die because he was gay!

Recently I've nearly come to regret telling them the story. I spent years of my childhood grappling with the impending loss of a parent—with death that comes after a long and difficult period of uncertainty. Why couldn't I have spared my children this bitter reality a while longer?

Yet they would have known anyway. Just as I knew the truth of my father's situation when I saw the pill bottles on the dresser, our children *know*, no matter how reassuring we think we are being with our words. I've lost track of the number of mothers in my Facebook groups posting about their children having tantrums, resisting bedtime, acting out. We rushed my own daughter to the ER four weeks ago because her pediatrician was convinced she had appendicitis. She didn't. She had severe constipation most likely brought on by stress.

Yesterday she and her five-year-old brother constructed a hospital in our living room where they treated a doll named Lily who was suffering from appendicitis and a broken leg. After some "blood work," Lily was revealed to have COVID-19. As I watched my children lovingly fashion an IV out of a science kit test tube and piece of packing tape, I was reminded of how desperately we all want to solve this. We want a way to fix it and make it go away—or to pretend it's not so bad.

Yet one thing the AIDS crisis taught us is that denial of the truth only makes the reality worse. The first cases of the virus that causes what would become known as AIDS appeared among gay men in the late 1970s. By 1982, roughly one thousand gay men had died and the Centers for Disease Control had coined the term "acquired immuno-deficiency syndrome" (AIDS) to describe the final stage of HIV infection. That same year, President Ronald Reagan's press secretary, Larry Speakes, dismissed questions about the growing epidemic, saying the White House knew nothing of the "gay plague." The current CDC director Robert Redfield—key to the nation's efforts to contain the coronavirus—was also part of the AIDS denial movement in the 1980s, helping to establish bigoted HIV policy within the U.S. Army, where he was a researcher. It was not until 1985 that Reagan first publicly acknowledged the AIDS crisis, at which point more than fifteen thousand Americans had died, most of them gay men.

Today we are witnessing another kind of bigotry leading to disproportionate loss of life: entrenched inequalities mean it's harder for people of color in the United States to work from home, less likely that they will have adequate health care and coverage, and more likely that they suffer from serious preexisting conditions. Disproportionately Black counties have accounted for 60 percent of coronavirus deaths so far.

As with AIDS, this pandemic reveals not only the reality of our universal mortality but also the lack of a cohesive social fabric. The rallying cry "We'll get through this together" demands that we embrace togetherness while highlighting our failure to forge *true* togetherness. Yet it has become the only truth I can offer my kids, a truth radically embraced and lived by gay people as they watched their world permanently altered by disease as leaders stood by, deeming their lives unworthy of sufficient intervention.

In the face of death, we tell stories of what we hope we can become. Just as it is powerful to think joy might stop HIV from binding to a cell, so too it is galvanizing to imagine that this virus might lead to a deeper togetherness—the most vital remedy we could manufacture, if (as history suggests) the most unlikely. Lately I've been reading John Ashbery's stunning AIDS poem, "How to Continue," an elegy for members of the Fire Island gay community of the Pines and Cherry Grove, where I spent summers as a child, many of whom died at the virus's peak:

> And when it became time to go
> they none of them would leave without the other
> for they said we are all one here.

If only it were so. Maybe one day it will be.

Prelude

Rowan Ricardo Phillips

I

My grandmother saw it coming and left.
I'd already left. It came late and swift
Like a tidal wave mistaken for a wave,
Came, not as a note but as an octave,
Black-keyed and mangled, searching the hospice
Only to find she'd left without notice,
The soul clapped from her body, masked by death,
Death hiding death from death and, finding no
Sign of her in the high cheekbones or skin,
Strode out on a cough into the evening.

II

In the weeks between her death and being
Laid to rest, life became COVID-19.
Both the living and the dead shared one air.
Then the service came, and I was not there.
I watched from the safe distance of an app
As my mother and uncle, masked among
The masked few in a pewless space, made peace

With the orphans who'd come to take their place.
Looking at them on-screen was like looking
Out at the world through the bars of a cage.

III

And now, high on a slope near Van Cortland,
The immortelles of perfect pitch sing Ena
Harris to sleep. Her shade goes there to listen
Bathed in the scent of ilex, palm, linden,
Kapok. It is Easter and she is dressed
In her lilac best and hat her daughter
Crossed bridge and Bronx and plague to bring to her.
She is two steps ahead of this pentameter
As it follows her through the flexed valley
Of the shadow of death; this elegy
Which, like all of them, is so useless and late.
My grandmother saw it coming. And she left.

Get the Shovel

Kathryn Lofton

When I was a child, my father hunted small game from the back door of our home, a narrow house surrounded by other houses and duplexes in a midwestern city. He sometimes boiled the carcasses in the garage so he could reconstruct the animals' skeletons, bleaching the bones and carefully wiring together the parts into lattice sculptures. Sometimes he had no plans for artistry, just killing the animals to rid his yard of intrusion. These bodies he buried at the bases of trees and bushes at the border of the lawn during the darkest part of the night.

Once, when I was eight, I thought he had killed a tabby that occasionally accompanied me for half a block as I walked to school. I waited until he went to the hardware store, maybe two weeks after the suspected crime, and dug up the freshest grave in the backyard. I exhumed the body, intending to say a proper good-bye. Maybe too I wanted to know the full measure of my father's menace. When I got to the body, the smell was so awful I threw up my lunchtime sandwich. I scrambled to rebury the creature and spray down my sick, reconstructing the scene so my father would not guess at my investigations.

It wasn't the tabby. Still, as I raked the dirt back over its body, I sang "Edelweiss" from *The Sound of Music,* which I decided was the most solemn song I knew.

Every child knows that when something dies it should receive a funeral.

Sociologists have explained repeatedly that theorizing society necessitates theorizing ritual. Ritual is the mechanism by which society understands itself, knows what it is, and restates what it wants to support or decry.

Three months into the pandemic, I have been invited to a lot of rituals even as I shelter in place. I've been invited to rabbinical and priestly ordinations of former students via Zoom. Friends have requested my attendance at virtual Passover meals; a colleague asked that I join a virtual church service to hear her preach. The Committee on Jewish Law and Standards in Conservative Judaism has offered guidance for remote gatherings in the time of COVID-19, including the recitation of the mourner's Kaddish. I've read about people managing to hold weddings in spite of the shutdown.

I wonder how some rituals can be made possible, and why others can't.

Funeral homes resort to storing bodies on ice; bodies pile up in trucks; bodies overflow morgues. "We can't properly bury our dead because of the situation," people are saying. And I think: Is that true? If a funeral is a ceremony that honors the dead, do the conditions of the pandemic preclude us from conducting them? And what does it mean if we can't hold these rituals?

I turn to the experts to help answer these questions, those people in forensic science and crisis management who have faced these logistics before. I read about mortuary provision in major accidents, natural disasters, or acts of hostility that cause mass fatalities. I read an article titled "Steadily Increasing Control: The Professionalization of Mass Death" in the *Journal of Contingencies and Crisis Management* that explains, "Today, as well, the handling of large numbers of bodies—and their personal effects—has become a specialized business."

I read, too, "Memorial services are an important step in the process of handling of the dead." In a 2015 article in *Disaster Medicine and Public Health Preparedness,* the authors emphasize, "Two of the most enduring American values are respect for the deceased and compassion for the bereaved."

According to the experts, if we can provide funerals, we should provide funerals. It's not logistics that keeps us from saying prayers or finding ways to gather together socially. It is our society, or present lack thereof. It is hard to make a ritual when you don't know what society you feel good about constituting.

I read a study about early medieval plague graves in Germany and find that, when people buried the victims, they observed the customary rites of burial. Plague bodies were dressed according to custom and given the same religious grave goods as those who died of other causes. The article is largely boring—DNA testing on soil samples, and so on—but then the authors get political, insisting that these medieval plague gravesites are not "mass graves":

> Usually, the term "mass grave" includes the perception of a certain way to conduct burials, like to bury the dead hastily, and with very minimalistic or no burial rites. Therefore, we would like to distinguish between "mass graves" and "multiple burials." Both can be the physical or material expression of a plague outbreak and therefore a higher rate of mortality, but they show a very different way of handling the crisis by the contemporary society.

A very different way of handling. The difference is in whether you're driven by haste or still observing the ceremonial rites. Mass graves exist when we want to move quickly, when we want to bury the mess without remark, when we can't handle speaking aloud the society that made this loss on this scale.

We are running mass graves on Hart Island.

I read about the purchase of the island, off the northeastern tip of the Bronx, in 1868 by the Department of Charities and Correction. I read about how the department bought it with the intention of setting up a workhouse for older boys from the House of Refuge on Randall's Island.

I think about the conjunction of those words: *charities* and *correction* and *refuge*.

I read about how, soon after the workhouse opened in 1869, the city began conducting the burials of unclaimed and unidentified people there. I look at photographs by Jacob Riis: of the dock where the unknown dead were unloaded, of the laborers loading coffins into an open trench at the city burial ground. I read about how, more than a century later, AIDS victims were buried on Hart Island in a cordoned-off corner; I read about how Rikers Island prisoners worked then and now as gravediggers; I read about the dizzying rates of infection and death from the coronavirus on Rikers Island. I read about how NYU's medical school buried donated bodies on Hart Island against the stated wishes of the donors. I read an apology from NYU: "As an institution, we weren't aware that this was happening," Lisa Greiner, a spokesperson for Langone Medical Center, said in 2016.

I read about what it means to be what law enforcement calls an "unidentified decedent" and what it means to identify one. I think about how an unidentified decedent is, by his, her, or their very deposit in a potter's field, marked by other identifiers: opioid addict, orphan, runaway, homeless, murder victim, plague victim. Subjects of charity all.

Funerals vary across cultures, but all societies discovered through archaeology and every culture engaged by anthropology share one idea: funerals symbolize the endurance of society and its values in the face of individual death. They symbolically conquer death by engaging the bereaved in a ritual that binds them together in the world of the living.

Can we have a society without funerals? The history of history, the history of sociology, the history of religions say: no.

As the death count in the United States approaches ninety thousand, I read a study about recovering from mass death. Cambodian survivors of the Khmer Rouge describe many PTSD symptoms, including recurrent, disturbing dreams about loved ones who died violently, and *kut caraeun,* or "thinking too much" about upsetting topics, traumatic events from the past, and the loss of loved ones. Kut caraeun can lead to headaches, dizziness, "wind attacks," depletion of bodily energy, heart weakness, and even "overheating of the brain," the crucial signs of which are memory loss and insanity.

The only durative therapies for survivors' suffering are Buddhist practices, including meditation; assisting the dead toward rebirth by honoring the dead person's merit; and participating in *p'chum ben,* the annual festival of the dead. As one male survivor reports, "We do rituals to calm the spirits of the dead, and I think that the ceremony can also calm down my feeling, so that I am not furiously mad at the cruel behavior of the Khmer Rouge."

I think about whether we can make up rituals to ease our own ritual failure. After World War II, local civilian committees across Eastern Europe excavated mass graves. Sometimes they did so under the enforcing eye of occupying forces. Sometimes they did so voluntarily. I think about these acts of exhumation: about how the townspeople then buried the remains of the bodies individually. I wonder if any of them got sick, or cried late into the night about what they had experienced. I think about how we do small things—read a poem, say a prayer, leave a token—not because we aren't collapsing but to remember someone lost as someone particular.

I think of a program in Bernalillo County, New Mexico, that pays for burials and memorial services for people whose unidentified remains have been in the county's possession for at least two years. I think of a headstone the county placed in the multiple burial site in 2012: "We grow afraid of what we might forget. We will find peace and value through community in knowing that we belong to each other."

I think about what I could do. I think about the old shovel I dragged out to dig for the tabby, and I think about the shovel I have in my basement now. I think of how I could get in a canoe and paddle from New Haven to Hart Island. I think about how, even though I lack upper body strength or seafaring experience, I could ride the rip, passing Bridgeport and Norwalk and Port Chester on my right, with Long Island a long sliver on my left. I could paddle until I find the island right at the juncture where Connecticut meets the Bronx, just before Long Island Sound becomes the East River.

I think I could do this. I think I should. Every burial deserves a song.

Provision

Monica Ferrell

For a long time I fed the children
From that inexhaustible larder
Money offers

But with the stores depleted
It now appears there's only one well
Here that never runs dry,

Just one bulb in this house
That never goes out
Even in the hoarse, bluey

Hour when dawn spreads
Toward the horizon's
Bald patch of trees,

When my earliest chorister
Leaps in the crib
And begins her orisons

Reaching out for this flawed
And dotted coastline
On which she'll press her lips

To drink not milk
But time through a dark
Nipple.

The Hour between Dog and Wolf

Monica Ferrell

Is it just me or is this wine
Terribly bitter
Which I'll drink anyway
To dissolve the bad

Aspirin of day
That did nothing for any headache,
Merely scratched at my throat like chalk.
The weather has turned.

Lately the dead spoil
In a van outside the morgue,
Filling the air with rumors
Thick enough the neighbors complain,

While an inmate cuts out holes
For a stranger in an island where no one goes.
We'll have to devise a new method
Of weighting bodies down with stones

So they can't return
Asking the same unanswerable
Question of those who failed
Them, yet keep going in this world.

The Jail Crisis

Russell Morse

Early in the outbreak, on the day Dr. Ross MacDonald, the head of Correctional Health Services in New York City, warned that a COVID-19 "storm" was coming to the city's jails, I went to Rikers Island to visit Ms. Mendez, a client of mine (some names have been changed to protect the individuals' privacy). Ms. Mendez, who had been at Rikers for months, had a health condition that made her vulnerable to infection. I needed her to sign a release authorizing me to get her medical records so I could try to get her out of jail before she contracted the virus.

As part of my work for a Manhattan public defender's office, I go to Rikers at least once a week to interview clients to help me prepare biographies for the court. Our clients include war refugees, chess champions, and Ivy League dropouts. Many have histories of mental illness, homelessness, substance abuse, and/or severe trauma. Most live in poverty, many are homeless, and the vast majority are Black or Latino. The details of my clients' lives help provide context for why they're in the system. Sometimes the narratives I prepare result in a better outcome: drug treatment, mental health support, twenty-five years instead of life. Just as often, they don't.

Since the start of the outbreak, we have focused our efforts on securing the release of medically vulnerable people. We identify which clients are at risk, obtain medical records to verify our claim, and schedule court appearances to request their release.

Even before MacDonald's urgent warning, my colleagues and I knew that Rikers would be the epicenter of the epicenter of the COVID-19 crisis. Jails are practically designed to allow infectious diseases to flourish: people live in close quarters, sharing facilities, with no protective equipment and without adequate health care. MacDonald compared Rikers to a "cruise ship recklessly boarding more passengers each week." Throughout the crisis, we have watched the infection rate climb until it reached its peak: one in ten people infected. That's 10 percent. The infection rate for New York City as a whole, even at its worst, was 2 percent.

Like most of my colleagues, I do this work because I believe that mass incarceration is the most pressing issue of our time. And I came to it because I am a formerly incarcerated person: I know this system's dangers and horrors because I spent years of my life living in these institutions.

Our office's mission is to provide holistic defense, which means, in part, that we provide each client with a social worker to help that client address the root causes—usually addiction, mental illness, and/or unemployment—of his or her entry into the system. Our clients' struggles are not over once they resolve a criminal case; we try to connect them to support services so they can get the help they need and avoid future arrests. Holistic defense was a revolutionary idea when it was introduced, but it has caught on, and many public defender practices now employ social workers.

At the beginning of the pandemic, the task of getting people out of jail was exciting: we prepared bail applications on the fly, gathered medical records and data about the infection rate at Rikers, and fought to get people released. Some of our clients have gotten out; others have not. (One judge, appearing on Skype in a cardigan against the backdrop of his home library, denied our application, saying, "It seems like they have things pretty well under control at Rikers." On the day of that hearing, the infection rate in New York City jails was more than 8 percent, with 334 known cases.) But even when we got them out, we realized, there was no longer anywhere for them to go.

AS THE CORRECTIONS OFFICER scribbled my name in a tattered visitors' log, I watched a coyote stroll along the road to the bridge, stopping to urinate on the "Welcome to Rikers Island" sign before ducking back into the bushes.

The coyotes showed up a few years ago. Unlike everyone else at Rikers, they move freely back and forth over the Rikers Island Bridge, usually in search of food. Some of the corrections officers feed them scraps when they see them in the parking lot: Styrofoam containers of pork-fried rice and pizza crusts. There used to be a colony of feral cats at Rikers, and the officers would put out food and water for them, too. Since the coyotes showed up, though, I haven't seen many feral cats.

The officer slid me a laminated pass to display on my car through the metal drawer. The air was thick with the scent of fake tropical fruit. The officers' bungalow is next to a waste-processing plant, so they burn scented candles in their cramped office—glass drums of crème brûlée, island breeze, and mango pineapple—to mask the smell of raw sewage.

That day in mid-March there were already seventy-five known cases of COVID-19 at Rikers, but this information hadn't reached the world beyond the institution. All we knew was that a few corrections officers had tested positive. Nobody in my office had tried to visit a client at Rikers since the start of the outbreak.

"Is there any restriction on counsel visits because of the virus?" I asked.

Scanning my paperwork, the officer shrugged. "Not that I know of, but they don't tell us anything." He handed my documents back and smiled. "Be safe."

Ms. Mendez is a forty-six-year-old woman who grew up on the Lower East Side. When I saw her in the visit booth, she wasn't wearing any protective gear. I could hardly hear her through the thick glass, so I raised my voice to tell her that we were trying to get her out because her medical condition put her at an elevated risk of death if she contracted the virus. She was living at the Rose M. Singer Center (the women's jail at Rikers, familiarly known as "Rosie's"), in an open dorm with dozens of other women, all sleeping a few feet from one another.

"Good," she exhaled, putting her long black hair up in a bun. "This building is infected. My old unit was shut down because a lot of the girls in there were sick. There's a girl in quarantine now; I used to sleep next to her in the dorm."

I asked Ms. Mendez to tell me about her life so that I could write a biography for the court. She told me that she grew up in public housing on Delancey Street with an abusive, alcoholic father, but that she had liked school, and she was the first in her family to go to college. "I studied child psychology because I was a sad kid and I wanted to know why life was the way it was and why people acted the way they did."

After graduation she worked for the city as a caseworker, helping people with HIV find housing. In her twenties she got into a relationship with an abusive, controlling man who followed her to and from work every day and beat her every night. At age thirty, worn down by the relationship, she started using cocaine and heroin after a friend introduced her to the drugs. "Ever since then, the handcuffs never came off." She held her arms up with her wrists pressed together and shrugged.

She signed a release so that I could request her medical records. Before I left I told her that we would do our best to get her out.

"You'd better hurry," she said. "It's getting worse in here every day."

I boarded the corrections bus for the parking lot. A static-filled version of "We Are the Champions" blasted through the speakers as we raced through stop signs. (Rikers bus drivers always run the stop signs.)

On the drive to the parking garage, I got a call from André, a client who'd just been released from Rikers. He'd been homeless for years, living on the streets ever since he aged out of foster care, and he has a serious mental illness. He was calling because he had gone to a resource center for people with mental illness after he was released only to learn that it was closed indefinitely due to the outbreak. He wanted to know where he could go. I didn't have an answer for him. The consistent messaging during this crisis has been that the best thing everybody can do is stay home. The closest thing to a home André has is the ancient history section at the Strand Bookstore, where he sits and reads for hours every night. The only homeless resource I knew that was open during the crisis was the Bellevue Men's Shelter, so I reluctantly suggested he go there.

One week later Ms. Mendez was released from Rikers in the middle of the night with a Metrocard and a winter coat. I don't know how she is doing now.

THE HALLS of the Manhattan criminal courthouse, usually a hive of confusion and chatter, were silent and empty the day I went to fetch my client Ms. Beckett. All nonessential functions of the court were suspended until further notice. A small sixty-year-old woman with a hunched back and a shock of white hair, Ms. Beckett had been approved for residential drug treatment and was scheduled to be released to her program that day. We had no way of knowing whether getting a sixty-year-old mentally ill woman out of Rikers in the midst of a pandemic was considered essential. Nobody we asked seemed to know, either.

My job was to appear before the judge and state that I would escort Ms. Beckett to her drug program directly from court.

I met my supervisor outside the courtroom before we went in. "I have to ask you," she said, "do you feel comfortable doing this?"

I knew what she was asking me. Ms. Beckett was coming from Rosie's, which already had several confirmed cases of COVID-19; it was very likely that she had contacted the virus. If I said no, she wouldn't be released. I nodded, and we walked into the courtroom together.

After the judge agreed to Ms. Beckett's release, I went to the first floor of the courthouse to wait for her. An hour later the officer stepped from behind the bulletproof glass and called to me down the hall. "They're releasing her now," she yelled. "But not through here. You have to go in the back where the buses are." The back of the courthouse is a loading dock where court employees take quick smoke breaks; it was obvious that the corrections officers wanted to have as little contact with Ms. Beckett as possible.

As I waited the dented metal door opened, and a young man wearing khaki jail clothes walked out with his arms outstretched and his face upturned to the sky. He got down on his knees in the rain and kissed the sidewalk, then stood back up. With the ceremony over, he looked around for a minute, as if he didn't know where to go next. Then he jogged down the middle of an empty street into Chinatown.

Moments later Ms. Beckett walked out, smiling when she saw me. She was carrying two large, clear garbage bags full of her belongings from Rikers: books, clothes, paperwork, and dozens of small bags of Cheetos and Bumble Bee tuna from the commissary. "Can you help me with one of these bags?" she asked. "I told them I wasn't leaving Rikers without my stuff."

The bag was heavier than I expected. I scanned the contents through the plastic: romance novels, a few letters, socks and underwear, bottles of shampoo and conditioner. She had spent so much time at Rikers that she had started to make a life there, collecting necessities where she could, and she didn't know when or how she would be able to replace these precious items once she was released.

It was early in the pandemic, long before we were all wearing masks and gloves and staying several feet apart. I had no protective gear, and neither did Ms. Beckett. I knew we'd be spending the day together in cars and waiting rooms, so I resigned myself to whatever might come of it.

She thanked me as I hoisted the bag. "Now let's go get some cigarettes."

Ms. Beckett looks older than she is—she's frail and her dark, weathered face is framed by wiry white eyebrows—but she hoisted the second bag effortlessly over her shoulder, leading the way to the deli around the corner. The man behind the counter wore a mask, still a rare sight at the time, and handed me a pack of Newports and a lighter for her.

In the car I called the people at the drug program to let them know we were on our way. The intake person interrupted me to say, "As of this morning, because of the public health crisis, we are no longer accepting new clients."

I tried to bargain, but it was clear that the order had come from above. Several agencies had already stopped accepting clients from Rikers as a precaution. I hung up the phone and told Ms. Beckett we couldn't go to Samaritan Village.

"Well, I'm not going back to Rikers!" She shook her head and raised her eyebrows, nervously fumbling with her bags, which she had refused to place in the trunk.

I explained that this wasn't going to happen, but that we did need to make a plan for her: a place to stay, a different program to go to, and a way to get her mental health medication. She said she could stay with her mother, so we headed there first.

Ms. Beckett's mother lives on the top floor of a public housing building in Harlem. Her nephew, clearly not expecting any visitors, answered the door. Ms. Beckett rushed inside without saying hello, still toting her garbage bag, and I followed her with the other bag.

The apartment was dark and stuffy. A dog barked from the back room. I followed Ms. Beckett into a cluttered bedroom, where her mother—a smaller, frailer woman in oversized pajamas—was sitting on the side of the bed next to an open container of Chinese food. Ms. Beckett put her bag down and hugged her mom, who slowly lifted her arm to return the embrace.

"I'll be right back, Mama."

Though she had been in jail for months, and nobody was expecting to see her that morning, she didn't linger for a reunion because she was afraid of being returned to Rikers. Once her bags were set down, we left the apartment.

I was surprised and sad that she hadn't stayed to spend time with her mother and nephew, or even to sit on the couch and put her feet up. Her only priority was following through on the requirements of the court.

We drove to the sole outpatient program I could find that was still accepting clients from Rikers. It happened to be on a block in

Harlem where Ms. Beckett had lived for years. "That was my window right there on the ground floor," she said, pointing to the projects across the street. "And that building right there—I watched my cousin jump out the window on the tenth floor. He landed right here." I looked down as we walked past the spot. She was unfazed.

A woman with long braids at the program office's front desk handed Ms. Beckett a clipboard, then called upstairs to the billing department. After a short conversation, she hung up the phone and looked at me, shaking her head. "Her Medicaid won't cover outpatient treatment, so we can't take her."

People lose their Medicaid coverage while incarcerated, and it has to be reactivated after they're released—a bureaucratic mess in the best of times. We walked back to the car and headed to the Medicaid office. Ms. Beckett was undaunted by the rejection and had already shifted her focus to the next hurdle.

As we drove through Harlem, she was shocked at how many people were in the streets. "Don't they know there's a virus out here?"

At Rikers she'd watched the news every night and knew more about the pandemic than I did. She shook her head. "Some people don't think shit stinks until you hit 'em in the face with it."

We arrived at the benefits office to find the doors locked. A notice on the glass informed us that the office was closed due to the pandemic. People were advised to call an 800 number. We went back to the car to phone, waiting on hold for nearly an hour.

I wasn't sure how much more I could do to help Ms. Beckett, but it didn't feel right to just leave her at her mother's house and tell her to keep calling the 800 number until she got through. I wanted to see the process all the way through with her, but I knew we had more dead ends ahead of us and a limited amount of time.

Even if we couldn't get her Medicaid sorted out that day, Ms. Beckett needed her mental health medication. In the past she'd gone to Harlem Hospital, which called in her prescriptions to a pharmacy. But she'd never tried to do that in the midst of a pandemic.

The doors to Harlem Hospital were blocked; out front a group of health care professionals in masks, hoods, and gowns asked people what they had come for. Ms. Beckett told them she needed her psychiatric meds, and they gave her a flyer with another 800 number on it.

Ms. Beckett registered neither surprise nor dismay. She thanked the woman who handed her the flyer, folded it, and put it in her pocket. She told me she had some old medication at her mom's house, so I gave her a ride back.

It was late in the day. I told her to call the 800 numbers and that I would work on getting things straightened out with the courts. She thanked me for the cigarettes before getting out of the car and running across the street into her mother's building.

Weeks after her release, Ms. Beckett called to tell me that she hadn't received her Social Security check. Those benefits are also deactivated when a person is placed in custody, and she couldn't reach anyone via the phone to reactivate them. Social Security (SSI) is her only source of income, and she told me she didn't have money for food or toiletries. I told her I would try to find a way to help her.

Two days later she was arrested for shoplifting at a drugstore near her home.

After years of doing this work, I am accustomed to the disappointment that comes with a client's rearrest. But this felt different. Ms. Beckett had tried to do everything she was asked to do. She had complied with her remote treatment requirements, called social services every day, taken her mental health medication, and not used drugs. She was arrested because the government agency that provided her only source of income didn't have a crisis plan in place to help people who depended on it. I don't know what Ms. Beckett was accused of stealing, but I imagine it was something similar to the items in her Rikers garbage bag: snacks, toiletries, maybe a romance novel.

A FEW DAYS LATER a client named Mr. Bey called me. In January, while at Rikers for a parole violation, he'd had emergency spinal surgery. His doctors said he was lucky to be alive, and it would be a miracle if he walked again. We'd been working to find a nursing home for him so he could recover from his surgery somewhere other than Rikers. Although we know now that Mr. Bey was lucky that nursing homes don't like to take people from jail, unfortunately, this meant that he had to recover in the infirmary at Rikers, which is where many of the early COVID-19 patients at the jail were housed.

In normal times the infirmary (NIC, or Northern Infirmary Command) is quiet. A client who broke his ankle playing basketball at Rikers one summer told me he preferred NIC because it had fewer fights and it's the only building at Rikers with air-conditioning. But in the early days of the pandemic it became overcrowded as jail administrators made a panicked plan to isolate (and concentrate) people who were infected. Mr. Bey had to speak loudly to be heard over the yelling in the background.

I could hear the panic in his voice. I naïvely asked him what it was like in the infirmary.

"Fear, chaos, confusion, pandemonium!" he said, his voice urgent. He was surrounded by people with flu-like symptoms all day, he told me, all sharing a small bathroom and one phone, with no protective gear or hand sanitizer. He was convinced that he would die, but he was so desperate to talk to us that he risked using the phone.

The first Rikers COVID fatality, Michael Tyson, was a man in his fifties who was jailed for failing to report to his parole officer, a minor infraction similar to the reason for Mr. Bey's incarceration. His death came a week after Governor Andrew Cuomo announced that the state agency that oversees parole would release low-level violators in the interest of public health. Mr. Tyson's release was held up by the review process, and he died shortly after being moved to the Bellevue Prison Ward.

Mr. Bey's release was held up for similar reasons. The courts were willing to let him serve his sentence in the community provided that he had a reentry plan. I worked to present a plan to the judge, prosecutor, and representatives from the parole board. He would live with his cousin in the Bronx, report to a parole officer regularly, and engage in treatment for substance abuse. We were able to make a convincing pitch, and Mr. Bey was scheduled for release.

Mr. Bey got out in late April, on the day the infection rate at Rikers passed 10 percent, and called me from a LinkNYC phone. I thought he was calling to share his relief at being released; instead, he told me he'd just come from Bellevue Men's Shelter. He was more agitated than when he'd called me from Rikers. "It's worse than Rikers in there! They had us all in the same waiting room with no masks, no nothing; people were smoking crack and K2 while they waited!"

His parole officer hadn't let him stay at his cousin's house because the officer hadn't performed a site visit yet. Instead he sent Mr. Bey to Bellevue Men's Shelter, the processing center for all the city's homeless services. Even in normal times I am reluctant to send clients to Bellevue Men's Shelter, a dumping ground for people the system has failed their entire lives: mentally ill, drug-addicted, destitute men who have run out of all other options. It is a violent, cramped sorting office where men wait to be sent out to other violent, cramped places (most of them on Wards Island). Bellevue Men's Shelter was unsanitary before the virus. I can only imagine what Mr. Bey walked into that day.

I asked him if they were doing anything to keep people safe.

"Let's be serious," he told me. "Hell no, they're not keeping people safe here."

Mr. Bey returned to Bellevue Men's Shelter the next day because he was homeless and had nowhere else to go. They placed him in another shelter in the Bronx, and just as he was settling in there, inspectors came and found that the conditions (crowded rooms, shared facilities) were unsafe. Mr. Bey and the other men in his shelter were moved to a hotel downtown. Since then he's been doing well: he found a full-time job working as a porter, and when we talk he is brimming with gratitude and optimism. But Mr. Bey is doing well because he's a resilient person, not because of anything the system did for him.

Like most of my clients, Mr. Bey has been failed by the system at every turn. While thousands of people were getting sick and dying, the system did what it's always done: ignored the needs of the most vulnerable among us. In a time of crisis, they have remained our lowest priority.

Coronavirus and the Danger of Disbelief

Randi Hutter Epstein

In late February I was at a dinner party on the Upper East Side of Manhattan. The media had reported the first death from coronavirus in the United States only two days earlier. Naturally, the conversation turned to COVID.

One of the guests, a librettist, mentioned that he heard that 40 to 70 percent of the world would become infected. An economist rattled off doomsday statistics and predicted imminent lockdowns. Then the host, an author, turned to me—I have an MD, though I'm not a practicing physician, let alone an infectious disease expert—and said, "Let's hear what the doctor has to say."

I can't remember my exact words, but I know I offered a sanguine assessment of the situation. An uptick of cases, perhaps. But not quarantines, school closures, or economic collapse.

Weeks later, in my restless quarantine half-sleep, I'd rehash my comments, cringing at the memory. How could I have gotten it so wrong? I had never been on the front lines of disease fighting, but I knew far too much about the history and epidemiology of pandemics to give such a misguided prognosis. It was almost as if the woman speaking with such confidence that evening was a different person from the one who had learned about infectious diseases in medical school. It was as if I lived in two realities: an intellectual self that could digest and dispense data, and an emotional self that couldn't grasp—couldn't take *in*—the import of that information.

IN THE 1980S, when I was a medical student at Yale, I spent many afternoons talking with renowned virus hunters Drs. Robert Shope and Wilbur Downs, professors of epidemiology and public health. We'd pack brown-bag lunches and sit around a conference table down the hall from the microbiology labs, home to a vast collection of viruses. The doctors regaled me with stories of adventure and lessons in public health, lessons I was eager to learn. They taught me that more soldiers during World War II were sidelined by germs than by battle injuries. They told me about tracking down Lassa virus in Nigeria, then studying the deadly germ back in a New Haven lab, where a few escaped droplets nearly killed a colleague. They taught me that, ironically, a victory in a public health campaign can be the reason for its demise. In the 1950s in Sri Lanka, for instance, an anti-malaria project reduced the number of afflicted people from more than a million to fewer than twenty. Funding agencies incorrectly deemed malaria vanquished for good, so aid was cut. Within a decade the germ resurged. The same thing happened in India and Bangladesh.

I came away from these discussions with an understanding of the urgent need for local teams around the world to surveil continually for lurking infections. Upon discovering an outbreak, these teams would alert a global network of experts who could help prevent the germ's spread.

In 1992, not long after I graduated from medical school, Dr. Shope and colleagues published an alarming National Academy of Sciences report, "Emerging Infections: Microbial Threats to Health in the United States." The report—which, once again, warned about the increasing possibility of global pandemics if precautions were not taken—got a lot of attention in the media. In one news conference, Dr. Shope warned that the world was still vulnerable to "something along the line of the 1918–1919 influenza pandemic that killed 20 million people worldwide."

In the aftermath of an Ebola outbreak in the mid-1990s, pandemics became fodder for literary blockbusters like Laurie Garrett's best-selling *The Coming Plague* (1994) and Richard Preston's *The Hot Zone* (1995), the latter turned into the Hollywood film *Outbreak,* starring Dustin Hoffman and Morgan Freeman. And just as Dr. Shope predicted, new viruses emerged: one after another, the world saw outbreaks of H5N1, West Nile virus, SARS, H1N1, MERS, Ebola (again), and Zika.

But none of this translated into a sustained policy response in the United States.

Bill Clinton, who held the presidency during the H1N1 and West Nile epidemics, created the National Pharmaceutical Stockpile (now the Strategic National Stockpile), but it languished under the administrations that followed. George W. Bush fired his biodefense czar during his first year in office (only to hire him back mere months later to lead bioterrorism preparedness programs after the anthrax attacks following 9/11). Obama mandated funds for a vaccine after H1N1 struck, but the vaccines weren't widely available until after the peak of the outbreak. In response to criticism, Obama's administration created a sixty-nine-page "Playbook for Early Response to High-Consequence Emerging Infectious Disease Threats and Biological Incidents." The Trump administration threw it out. Overall, the past twenty years saw a gutting of each initiative put in place to protect us.

Yet, even given all this, I'm embarrassed to admit I assumed that if a dangerous germ arrived on our shores, we'd have the infrastructure and organization to mobilize accurate testing, administer safe and effective treatments, and produce and distribute vaccines. Though

I knew about the threat of a pandemic—and about our fractured and reactive health care system—I had also read of triumphs. With vaccines we conquered smallpox and nearly eradicated polio. We developed drug cocktails that turned HIV infection from a death sentence to a chronic, undetectable disease. In the early days of coronavirus, these were the memories that surfaced in my mind. They were more comforting than the other story my intellect told.

THE PHILOSOPHER William James wrote that our concepts of the world are based not only on knowledge but also on our own lived experiences. He believed that no one grasps the full and true complexity of reality; we each create our own version without fully comprehending everyone else's. "We mutilate the fullness" of reality, he wrote, by confusing it with our own piecemeal experiences.

Perception is based on experience; we accrue memories by soaking in the sensory details of the world around us. These details seep into our brains and get categorized according to facts (stored in the hippocampi, seahorse-shaped organs on each side of the brain) and emotions (stored in the amygdala at the tip of the hippocampi). Data (the hippocampus stuff) without emotions (the amygdala part) are less likely to stick with us. If there's no memory, there's nothing to conjure up. Many of those in Wuhan during the initial days of the outbreak could recall the traumas of SARS, which hit southern China in 2002. That's what propelled Li Wenliang, a Wuhan ophthalmologist, to post warnings on social media of a potentially new and dangerous virus. (Dr. Li was criminalized for speaking out and died weeks later of COVID-19.) The SARS experience also may have helped East Asian countries respond more quickly and successfully to the pandemic than their Western neighbors. Recalling the emotional burden of the past shaped the way they responded to the present.

Similarly, our lack of experience with pandemics shaped how America responded—or failed to respond. Certainly it shaped how I responded. The disbelief that results from a lack of experience is different, I think, from doubt: James called doubt the "true opposite" of belief. Because disbelief happens when the mind is in unrest and struggling to perceive a complicated world, it's related to denial, which the twentieth-century psychoanalyst Anna Freud characterized as a way of blocking out unpleasant realities. I wasn't a pandemic denialist, nor did I doubt the facts. But without an image bank to draw on, I was—like many others—merely living in a state of suspended belief.

Of course, the hedging language of medicine may also have added to our collective incredulity. Although most of us crave certainty, scientists use qualifying words in the conditional tense, such as "may" or "most likely." They never promise. The ifs and buts of the medical discourse around an emerging virus leave a lot of wiggle room for an optimist like me. Maybe the bad stuff won't happen after all—even if it's "probable," it's not "guaranteed."

These days when I Zoom with doctor friends, I hear a lot of "we told you so's." I nod, but I feel like a fraud. On a recent episode of NPR's *Fresh Air,* John Barry, the author of *The Great Influenza*—a gripping narrative of the 1918 pandemic chronicling the many ways that both doubt and disbelief left an earlier nation unprepared—told Terry Gross that "intellectually understanding it is one thing and having it hit you is something quite different." When asked if he expected it, he replied, "Yes, and no." And I felt solace.

A DOCTOR once told me that everything is clearer with a "retrospectoscope": that it's much easier to see where things went astray in the past than to speak with any kind of certainty about the future. When it comes to public health issues, we may never be able to cultivate that full sense of reality, an ideal that William James considered unattainable anyhow. But we do need to make decisions based on data, shelving our personal sentiments of disbelief.

We need systems to assess the information and to prepare an infrastructure to combat diseases. We need to fine-tune our scientific communication so people believe the experts and heed their advice. Whether we can emotionally prepare may not matter. Whether we are wearing masks because we are afraid of spreading disease to loved ones or out of an abstract sense of civic duty may not matter. What matters is that we learn the lessons of a larger history—that we believe in them and prepare accordingly, even if we haven't lived through them.

I might be overthinking my own incapacity to grasp what was about to hit America. Last week I emailed my friend who hosted the dinner party. Perhaps I wanted to make light of my errant predictions; perhaps I wanted to apologize. He remembered the opera composer reciting statistics, but not the dire words of the economics professor. And, to my relief, he had no recollection of my comments—luckily they hadn't made an impression.

I've been walking around my neighborhood taking photos: masked shoppers separated by taped stripes six feet apart outside store entrances; masked and gloved Duane Reade employees behind blockades of plexiglass and empty crates. I've shot the "LIMIT: 2 EACH" placards leaning on toilet paper stacks and also the apology signs hanging on shuttered stores.

I want a visual record. I worry that what was once shock will become the new normal and vanish from my amygdala. Photographic proof may jiggle a few neurotransmitters. The act of taking pictures,

I hope, will sear the feeling of the empty streets into my brain cells. I want to commit this time to memory so that it will inform my perceptions of the future.

I want to remember that I was warned, but that I was stunned all the same.

Invisible Kingdoms

Noreen Khawaja

The soft prickle of Cynthia Ozick's voice flooded my ear pods as I walked along the creek at the park's northern end. In recent weeks this usually unpeopled zone had come to feel like the busy courtyard of a vast urban sanitarium. But today, for no evident reason, it was quiet. A friend had recommended the podcast to me, noting the ASMR-like effect of Ozick's voice. She was reading a story by Steven Millhauser about a master miniaturist appointed to the court of a fictional king. Each time she whispered the phrase "soo smaall," a tiny, buzzing cloud seemed to expand upward and then dissolve in a wondrous slowness.

In the story the Master, as the miniaturist is called, is working full-time on a marvelous toy palace commissioned long ago by the king's father. The palace has six hundred rooms, dungeons, and orchards and is large enough to require a real room of its own.

One day the Master is admiring a basket of apples he has made for one of the orchards—the bent wooden slats of the basket, the tiny wooden apples, "each no larger than the pit of a cherry," and, especially, a minuscule copper fly resting on the stem of one of the apples, with two delicate and consummately rendered wings. Instead of feeling pleased with this work, he shudders. Why should he stop there?

An opera of intensification ensues. First a much smaller version of the same basket, filled with even smaller apples. And the new fly—to the naked eye no more than a dark speck, but viewed with a magnifying lens just as meticulously formed as the last. Those who witness this miniaturized and magnified insect are astonished, even disturbed. The Master proceeds swiftly with more difficult miniaturizations: groups of animals carved from cherry pits; a wing of the toy palace, reduced in perfect detail, that fits beneath a thimble. Each task requires more elaborate tools of magnification, more controlled environments in which to work, pushing him into greater isolation and leaving refurbishment of the old toy palace for apprentices to manage. Until at last the yearning that has driven the Master from that first basket of apples arrives at its true object: what he desires is not a smaller world but to create in a zone of such exquisite subtlety that the distinction between visible and invisible itself becomes too fine to hold. He sets to work on "a world so small that he could not yet imagine it," a world that would be entirely, unmagnifiably, invisible.

At court dissent has been brewing for some time. The more devices required to view the Master's creations, the more his audience suspects him of playing tricks. Has he actually created a palace so small it can be viewed only with a series of optical aids? Or is it all just an elaborate illusion?

As his attentions turn from the infinitesimal to the invisible, the Master retreats almost entirely from court life. In a final scene, his former apprentices come to visit him, asking to see his mysterious new creation. The Master obliges, pointing to the work he has created as if it were like one of his former palace scenes, with elaborate details to be studied and admired. The apprentices pretend to pay their respects, murmuring politely. But they have actually seen nothing at all, and the Master understands that contempt brews within them. Lonely, longing to share, and yet realizing it is impossible, the Master returns to his great work, the invisible kingdom.

The reading ended. An advertisement came on for another podcast. A man's voice, bright and smooth: *This week on the* Radio Hour *two leading writers join us . . . the two great crises of our time . . .* The music faded in the background as an older man—leading writer number one, I presumed—began to speak at great volume, full of distress, exclaiming, *Science is real!* A breath later and louder, *Physical reality is real!* The words revealed the contours of an anxiety I did not know I had. Was this still part of the story? Is this what "an invisible kingdom" meant? That you might never know for sure where it was, or wasn't; *what* it was, or wasn't? The speaker's cries were followed by a rapid, imploring slush—*people . . . have got to realize . . . just because . . . it doesn't mean . . . our civilization . . . even the pandemic . . . what you can see . . . before it's . . .*

As I walked home, these two performances weighed on me. Between them a gap opened, which I tried to fill: the earnest science writer pleading for reality to be treated as real. The celebrated artist who'd given up every notion of ontological persuasion. The artist at the peak of his career, choosing to pass his prime in physical and emotional isolation, devoting himself to work in a world he would never be able to share. The science writer unprepared for his new problem: not one of distinguishing between truth and falsehood but of refashioning a voice for the truth, moving through (not against) its evolving fictionalization.

I shuffled through these slides faithlessly, attempting for obscure reasons to weigh the two characters equally, unable to shake the feeling that they were not equal, that the miniaturist knew something the climate writer did not. But what?

He knows that indexical gestures are inadequate to the task of conveying what is real. He knows you cannot just point at something and expect people to see what you see.

He knows that earnestness is dangerous. Maybe that's what court life teaches, life in the uneven currents of power and favor, skill and envy. In an epistemic crisis, it's the first thing they use against you.

And I thought something else—

Would the miniaturist even be on the science writer's side? He left the microscope behind, after all. But not for the same reason as others at court, who suspected it of working dubious tricks. For him, the reality of the microscope was not dubious *enough.* He wanted to work with what was truly ambiguous. If contingency means a thing could have been otherwise, ambiguity means it may be otherwise right now.

He knows, then, that the line between the real and unreal cannot be established securely. He knows that what is called unreal is never inactive. He knows its activity cannot be discovered by showing or telling. It is known by making, by attempting to make. Making reveals something that telling or showing does not.

Arriving home on a day far enough into quarantine that notions of "after" and "before" appear equally hypothetical, I wondered if the stakes of this ambiguity have simply become more apparent. How often does it happen, in less strung-out times, that we draw a particular boundary between reality and unreality, paying as little attention as possible to the feeling that it might just as well be drawn another way, or perhaps not at all? Once a day? Once a minute?

Listening to our media work out a way to talk about evidence right now—what we know and what we don't; what it means to know and not to know those things—feels a bit like watching someone extemporaneously translate Proust into a language with no grammatical tense. They relay the words the scientists offer up, but the sentences don't do the work we want them to. I think of Millhauser's miniaturist and I wonder: Why should a fictional artist, making worlds no one admits as real, have a better grasp of how power communicates than a public intellectual?

The question the science writer did not ask is what it takes for something to feel real. He attempts to show us that science *is* real, but what he wants is for us to *treat* it as real. He does not consider that these may be different tasks. And why should he? Speaking from a global pandemic, nestled in a culture war unfolding on a rapidly warming planet, who has time to worry about metaphysical questions like whether the quality of realness depends not only on facts but also on the work of a certain kind of atmosphere?

I do, it seems. This spring, as my institution transitioned to online instruction, I had been teaching a new graduate seminar, The Surreal. It primed me to notice how deeply the concept of surreality is woven into our experiences of this moment. The world outside looks like the dystopian dramas we've been watching for decades. The rector of St. John's watches from a Fox News TV studio as the president visits his church, where peaceful protesters have just been cleared out with tear gas and rubber pellets so that the president can pose for a photo op with the Bible. A Brazilian doctor struggles to cope as her neighbors engage in rapturous coronavirus-themed dance parties while her patients lack the sedatives necessary to be unconscious for their own intubation. When the term *surreal* is invoked in such cases, what it tracks is the uneasy proximity between present reality and what we expect to be a representative distortion. "Surreal" names a mode of life in which reality and representation relate in more complex ways than realist modes tend to allow for. The artisans of reality itself, we are learning, are not always realists.

We want a just world; we expect a just world to feel like a natural one, as though unforced. We seek to transform society consciously;

we despair of feeling that reality is orchestrated. Given all the inconceivable things human beings seem able to live with, our feelings about reality itself appear curiously brittle. Why has no one taught us to explore what truth feels like in a climate of heterogenous, unequal orchestration? The Master, of course, teaches no one. But he correctly assesses the barriers to persuasion. And Steven Millhauser creates an atmosphere in which it is possible to feel the power of that character's silence.

Perhaps I should not be expecting to encounter oracular poetry around every sonic bend. My friend describes this hope as a ringing in her ear, the dull itch of the present as it scrambles over itself, trying to catch up to futures that have yet to arrive.

JUNE

The Trees Witness Everything

Victoria Chang

Still Morning

No mornings are still.
The newly dead move the most.
They force flowers to dilate.

To Ashes

How many ashes
do I walk through in one day?
I have forgotten
where my mother's ashes are.
I think they are flushed
into the earth. Yesterday,
the crow gave me an
invoice for its signaling
of death—I owe one whole year.

To the Book

Here is March again.
An image is a shawl. Birds
are a transcript of our thoughts.

When You Go Away

I look at my hands,
watch how they bend, just like air,
can sit still like ice,
the small lines at the knuckles,
how they can drag hair,
or cover a woman's mouth.
I should have kept the
ashes of her hands to see
whether they could still be held.

Avoiding News by the River

All the announcements.
The mayflies land on a leaf.
No one there ever looks up.

White Morning

An oak tree must ache,
each year of desire in rings
or maybe nothing
hurts. Maybe all pain is joy.
Maybe joy is the
flare-up to be avoided.
Don't look at the bird
on the veranda singing
nothing to us or for us.

How I Became a Prophetess

Joyelle McSweeney

My first act of prophecy was to predict my own child's death.

In her prenatal scans, Arachne had looked perfectly healthy, but when she was born, she couldn't breathe. A chest X-ray showed white thick light instead of fat black air. Her guts had moved up to where her lungs should be. She was flown off to a NICU, where she died. Uncannily, in the years and months leading up to her ill-starred birth, I had written a book called *Toxicon*, replete with the themes of toxins, contamination, gestation, mutation, a smashed delivery suite, and a "pulseless fontanel." Arachne's birth converted *Toxicon* from a book of obsessions into one of prophecies.

And there, in the delivery suite, I was like Cassandra, the original prophetess, filling the air with my screams.

Let's begin again—*ab ovo*, as classicists would say. From the beginning. From the egg. Arachne was born with an unexpected birth defect, flew off to a NICU, lived thirteen days, and died. But I survived, much to my regret. I returned to the house without her. I was recovering from a C-section and two weeks on my feet in the NICU, my brain continuously bathed in cortisol and fluorescent light. Now, crossing the ten feet from the curb to the door with the news of her death inside me was the longest and strangest voyage of return. In some ways I have never completed this crossing.

I wanted to write a book that was like a quiver of poisoned arrows.

Now, like Zeno's arrow, I keep flailing and cannot arrive.

I spent a few months in a stupor. I would wake up thinking I was still pregnant, kept looking for the baby from the corner of my eye. But Arachne could not be retrieved, nor born a second time.

Instead, spring came.

I was furious at spring's arrival: its wealth, its wetness. Floribund and moribund, its swollen river, its pink flowers spattering down.

The shock of this fury was powerful. I began to write.

I wrote a book called *Arachne* over just a handful of weeks, odes and elegies and forgeries and true confessions. Together, the books are riven with biological catastrophes, viruses, gestations and mutations, police violence, ill-starred births and abundant, microbial growth: portent upon portent, star upon star. When spring was done, the work was done. I put down my pen.

The Rust Belt looks good in spring, even now, draped in that rotting garland. Runnels and rivulets. Each rill its drill of pain.

WHEN BOOKS OF PROPHECY are opened, we discover what we knew all along.

This is also true of coronavirus itself. When the black boxes of the death tallies were first opened and the disproportionate effects of the virus on Black, brown, and native people and communities were first brought to light, the results were a punch in the gut—breathtaking, dismaying, shocking—and then not shocking at all. The destruction and exploitation of communities of color, the perceived disposability of many kinds of laboring bodies, as well as those too weak, ill, or old to labor: these are the crimes our nation is built on, hardened into the structures of our politics and economy to this day. They underwrite the racial disparities in life expectancy, health outcomes, maternal mortality, lifetime earnings, policing and incarceration, voter suppression, and even access to food, health care, and clean air and water. Why should it be shocking to open the book of our present catastrophe and read the facts that were written there centuries ago?

It is the past, not the future, that prophecy brings to light.

What happened to Arachne was statistically unlikely, but fate's arrow still found its way across the cosmos to her impossibly small sac of cells. What's happened to America under COVID-19 was statistically likely: it is America itself. Our future is our past. For me individually, under the brainblow of Arachne's life and death, I can't form something shaped like hope. But I can admit to curiosity about nextness—next life forms, exchanges, translations, community configurations. I gaze on corporate platforms and can see the chains of knowledge and mutuality being recalled, reconfigured, and communicated like flickering, seizing strands of DNA, kissing and splitting, riven with radiance, mutation, exuberance, memory, and copying errors.

Something's there, right? Some monstrous, anachronistic nextness, a present moment pulsing with pasts and futurities, undead knowledges, arts, and technologies, maybe lawlessly, collectively gestating itself, writing the book of itself, looking forward and back, dreaming, remembering. Will it arrive too late or right on time? This counter-catastrophe—will it gestate forever? Or can it be born?

Lives or Livelihoods

Khameer Kidia

Mazoe cordial is an elixir named for the region of Zimbabwe with the sweetest oranges. Originally a luxury created by British colonists on the backs of locals, the orange concentrate has been reclaimed by Zimbabweans for ourselves. Mazoe now conjures childhood memories: birthday parties, soccer practice, or the reward dispensed by our school matron after a cross-country run. Those of us living in the diaspora risk spilling it in our suitcases for a few sips of home.

So during fieldwork at a rural health clinic earlier this year, I was confused that the staff seemed disappointed when I offered this token of appreciation. "We must mix it with water," said Agnes, a village health worker. Of course we must mix it with water, I thought; it's Mazoe. It took me a bit longer to realize that the issue was not the cordial but the lack of running water.

After troubleshooting with Agnes, we gathered an assortment of plastic vessels from around the clinic, loaded them into our truck, and drove the potholed dirt road to the nearest community well. "This well was donated by a local politician," Samuel, our driver, said. "He hoped to gain more votes in the next election." In 2008, four thousand Zimbabweans died of cholera from untreated drinking water, yet millions still lack access to clean water. My mother in Harare has her own well, which could supply an entire village. I tried to imagine a life dependent on the wealthy and corrupt for such a basic human right.

When I opened the truck door, empty Coke bottles fell out in an acoustic chord progression of hollow plastic thuds. A breeze from the grasslands carried the smell of imminent rain and reminded me how Zimbabwean summers fuse the ingredients of photosynthesis: thunderstorms and blinding sun. The metal pump handle was shiny—worn smooth from frequent use. Each morning women congregate around the well and wait their turn to fill their families' receptacles before a long walk home. They chat and laugh, clustered closely. Agnes and I, chatting and laughing too, filled each container to the brim, moistening the surrounding red soil until it was mud.

Back at the clinic, I marveled at the building's design, an open-air layout that was standardized for clinics across the country after independence. The clinic architects knew that confined spaces could spread tuberculosis, so some walls are porous—built of concrete blocks with flower-shaped empty spaces that allow breeze and light to fill the waiting area. On a grassy patch far from the tree bearing the sign "Coughing Zone," Agnes mixed the white man's Mazoe with the Black women's well water and poured the cold golden liquid for everyone. For a split second we forgot about cholera. We did not yet know a novel coronavirus would be arriving next month.

On our drive back through the lush bush, the skies burst open. The clinic blurred behind us as sheets of rain pressed through the concrete sieve walls, bathing the open waiting area. Samuel navigated the road's rapidly filling craters, barely able to see inches ahead. "There is plenty water," he explained, "just no plumbing."

I'M BACK IN BOSTON in March, and my hospital prepares for coronavirus. Heading into work, I ensure that my green N95 mask fits so snugly it hurts my face. I want it to. I want to be safe. The ICU where I work is windowless, without breeze or sunlight, but when I open the tap, water flows. I scrub my hands until they sting raw. We keep the tap running to wash the virus out of our scrubs and wipe it off the surfaces. I don and doff semi-transparent gowns, throwing them away each time I exit a patient's room. The nurses at the clinic in Zimbabwe pray for such luxuries.

Over the course of two weeks, we create two hundred new ICU beds with ventilators from the operating rooms and some older vents stored in the basement. By comparison, Zimbabwe has at most a hundred ventilators for its population of 14 million. Our bioethics committee deliberates ventilator rationing in the unlikely event that we run out of all two hundred. Should we give them to the young, the old, the sick, the healthy, the wealthy, the heroes?

They don't mention Zimbabweans. This week a man I went to high school with is the first Zimbabwean to die of coronavirus. He was the host of a prominent local TV show. Rumor has it his family searched in vain for a ventilator during his last hours. My mother lives in Zimbabwe; she is in her sixties with high-risk medical conditions. If she needed a ventilator, she would die too. I wish they could send just a few to Zimbabwe. Even the older vents from the basement.

Because of the time difference, my cell phone bleeps at odd hours as a deluge of WhatsApp messages arrives from family and health care colleagues back home. "How do we reuse our masks?" "Do we need running water?" "Can we use garbage bags instead of medical gowns?" I feel useless, unable to help, and embarrassed that my Boston hospital spent millions on a mask-decontamination machine. I suggest rubbing alcohol, if available. We share experiences from the front lines. I recommend testing patients twice, in case of false negatives. They tell me there aren't enough kits to test most patients once. Triage according to oxygen levels, I say. But rural Zimbabwe doesn't have the $10 pulse oximeters we use to measure those levels. Nevertheless, we all agree that the most effective strategy requires no additional resources: lay patients on their bellies; they will breathe more comfortably.

The Zimbabwean Ministry of Health releases its daily update. April 29: forty cases and four deaths—still early days. But if Zimbabwe reaches its predicted peak in July—winter and flu season—they won't have ventilators or clinical trials or heart-lung machines. In some hospitals they won't even have running water.

BY EARLY MAY there is an explosion of public health messaging in Zimbabwe, and people's lives have begun to change. Blue and yellow flyers with stick figures mime prevention strategies in Shona—*geza maoko* (handwashing), *vhara muromo* (cover your mouth), and *usaenda kana kugara pedyo nevamwe vanhu* (practice social distancing). None of the flyers explain what to do if you don't have running water or if you can't socially distance.

The Zimbabwean government—well versed in controlling its people—enforces a strict lockdown. My mother tells me that businesses use an infrared thermometer to measure the temperatures of those entering. A relative is turned away at a police roadblock and told she must shop at the store closer to home. A colleague texts me a photo of a fine he received for maskless driving. The police are emboldened; the consequences of violating quarantine become severe.

"People are starving to death," my mother argues over Skype when I praise the stringent lockdown. I feel a pang of guilt as I stare at my stimulus check. The cost of isolation is far greater in Zimbabwe. At the end of 2019—after Cyclone Idai killed more than a thousand people and left many more homeless—the country was facing the threat of a terrible famine; more than 7 million people, over half the population, had been forced into food insecurity. Most are street vendors, food stall owners, airtime salesmen. Without savings or refrigeration, they rely on short-term pay and daily visits to the market. Now their earnings have stopped and the markets are closed. There is no working from home, no stimulus check.

I picture Mbare, the open-air market closest to my home in Harare. Raw peanuts and spinach pile high. The aroma of roasting corn fills the air as men cluster around fires to scorch *chibage*—the white maize staple—until it is blackened on the outside and the kernels are tender enough to pluck. There is a racket of haggling and chatter and chickens. Women exchange banknotes carried in their blouses for purple sweet potatoes and handfuls of *mopane* worms. At this beloved crossroads, coronavirus will flourish. Yet the market is a lifeline. "The tension," a global health mentor writes via email, "is finding the right balance between lives and livelihoods."

As I click away from his email, wondering where this balance might lie, I stumble across a recent video on the Human Rights Watch website. Mothers and daughters gather at a well in Harare near my family home. It has a shiny pump handle like Agnes's. The women walk three miles for two *chigubus* (plastic containers) of water— barely enough to quench their husbands' thirst, clean their homes, and bathe their babies. They wait ten hours, sometimes overnight, in crowded queues. They cannot socially distance. They share the pump handle, but the ritual is different from the one I learned from Agnes. There is no chatting or laughing. For their families' only hope of sanitation, the women brave unsanitary conditions. They are trying to strike the same balance as the food vendors and market goers: death now versus death deferred.

Thucydides in Times of Trouble

Emily Greenwood

I have always found it hard to believe students and colleagues who say that Thucydides helped them through a crisis. In the first book of his *History* he announces a terse, uncompromising agenda, and the ensuing work is one long disenchantment with human affairs. But in the last three months, I have found a tenderer aspect of Thucydides. In the slow, turbid dive of the pandemic, Thucydides' account of the Athenian plague has been my distance line through the compound shocks of public catastrophe and private bereavement. And in the still greater depths of the urgent, unfinished history of racism that kills with both sly neglect and dehumanizing violence, I recall Thucydides' interpretation of another epidemic as a metaphor for the health of the body politic.

Thucydides died while still writing and editing his *History* of the Atheno-Peloponnesian War (431–404 BCE). For the Athenian Thucydides, the defining crisis of this war was a devastating epidemic that struck the city-state of Athens in the summer of 430 and intermittently ravaged the population for four years. Thucydides, who caught (and survived) the plague himself, relates that "an untold number" of Athenians died—perhaps as much as a third of the total citizen population. (This is itself a sobering reflection on the history of who counts as being countable in political communities, since Thucydides gives us estimated mortality figures for Athenian citizens only, neglecting to mention the effect of the plague on Athenian women and children, the large enslaved population, and the immigrant population in Athens.) Attempts to retrodiagnose the Athenian plague continue to this day (typhoid fever has been suggested), but Thucydides himself eschews any such identification, commenting that "the type of the disease exceeded explanation."

Instead he takes greater interest in the spectrum of human ingenuity and fallibility, particularly as revealed in responses to novel crises, from the way the mind struggles to take in sudden reversals of expectation to the limitations of leaders to respond and adapt to events.

Read today, his account of the plague's onset sounds familiar: the slow beginning as reports spread and then a sudden revolution of time as the inexorableness of the disease sank in. At the start Thucydides uses an ingressive past tense: "the plague first began to occur." This puts us in real time with the Athenians as cases begin to crop up and they begin to register the outbreak of the disease. To read this phrase a few months into our own pandemic is to experience an odd feeling of nostalgia as we remember ourselves back in early March 2020: on the threshold of an as yet ungraspable future, developing a sudden lay interest in epidemiology.

As Thucydides tells it, the Athenians first reacted to the plague by looking to contemporary medicine for answers that it could not give. He nods to the case histories of contemporary physicians who charted the progress of diseases by days, noting indicative signs and recording the outcome, whether recovery or death. We have an insight into these case histories from books 1 and 3 of the *Epidemics,* attributed to the famous physician Hippocrates. These books record communal patterns of disease by region and season as well as individual case histories in which the symptoms and course of the disease were atypical. From the sparse notes in the case history of a man named Erasinus, who lived on the island of Thasos, we read: "Fifth day. Early in the morning was composed, and completely lucid; but well before noon he became utterly delirious and lost control. His extremities were cold and bluish and his urine stopped. He died as the sun was setting" (my translation). The accounts of epidemics in the Hippocratic corpus are empirical in approach, interpreting and recording what happened as a resource for physicians practicing medicine in similar conditions and populations; although the accounts are dramatic, even fatalistic, the ordered chronology of the case history creates an impression of control.

In contrast, Thucydides gestures toward medical time only to illustrate the futility of calibrating a disease for which there was no diagnosis and no effective treatment, which had a very high mortality rate, and which ravaged even its survivors. Of the "progress" of the plague, Thucydides writes,

> Most either died from the internal burning on the ninth or seventh day, while they still had some strength, or if they survived and the disease descended into the belly, and severe ulceration occurred and completely liquid diarrhea set in at the same time, most perished later from the weakness this caused. . . . And if anyone survived beyond the most serious effects, the attack on his extremities at least made a mark. For it struck the genitals and fingers and toes, and many survived with these lost, some their eyes as well. Total loss of memory also came over some as soon as they recovered, and they could not identify either themselves or those closest to them.

In the gap where medicine falls short, Thucydides re-creates the psychological impact of the plague in precisely modulated prose. He considers the plague from three different prepositional angles: it falls *onto* the Athenians, *against* the Athenians, and they fall *into* it (*eispiptō, epipiptō,* and *peripiptō* in Thucydides' Greek). The assorted prepositional verbs are not just a case of an exacting writer mixing up his prose; rather, they suggest that the Athenians, in their distress, entertained several parallel explanations for their suffering all at once. The first two verbs—*eispiptō* (fall on, set upon) and *epipiptō* (attack)—are also used of military invasion and reflect the connection that the Athenians made between the Peloponnesian invasion of their land and the sudden onset of the plague. (This coincidence led to the conspiracy theory that the Peloponnesians had poisoned the water reservoirs in the Athenian port of Piraeus.) The third compound verb, *peripiptō* (fall into), bears connotations of hapless, blundering agency, and leaves open questions of causation and responsibility.

Like us, the Athenians simultaneously resigned themselves to the plague's onslaught and looked to hold political leaders accountable for decisions that contributed to their suffering. Chief among these was the war strategy proposed by the Athenian general Pericles, which involved evacuating Athens's rural townships and moving their residents into the urban center so that the entire population could shelter within the city's walls. This strategy led to overcrowding and increased transmission of the disease, forcing people to witness others' traumatic suffering at close quarters: "The devastation did not occur in an organized situation, but the dead and dying lay on top of one another, and half-dead men tumbled in the streets and around all the springs in their craving for water." In his description of the Athenians' anger toward Pericles, Thucydides again uses the verb *peripiptō:* "The Athenians held Pericles responsible as the one who had persuaded them to go to war and because they had fallen into misfortunes because of him."

Thucydides does not contradict this accusation, but he himself focuses more on collective responsibility, describing how the plague exposed weaknesses in social, cultural, political, and religious life, challenging the Athenians' sense of invulnerability and exceptionalism. In the *History*, the narrative of the plague follows and seems to answer the funeral oration for Athens's war dead delivered by Pericles, as well as an earlier speech by Pericles on war strategy in the lead-up to the war. Pericles' funeral oration glorifies Athens, boasting about the superiority of her democratic system of government, the quality of life enjoyed by Athenians (that is, free-born, adult male citizens), and the city's preeminent power. Although Thucydides does not describe the cause of Pericles' death in 429 BCE, his readers would have been aware that the general himself died of the plague.

The classicist Rachel Bruzzone has demonstrated that Thucydides' plague narrative itself belongs to an ancient Greek literary tradition, reaching back to Homer, of accounts of "a total and simultaneous breakdown on many fronts, social, natural, epidemiological, and political." In Thucydides' telling, the compound experience of war and epidemic leads to manifold desolation as the customary way of life and death collapses, and individual losses and grief keep piling up. The city falls into despair and anomie as people abandon hope for the future. The skeleton of society is exposed and time loses its disciplining hold on human life. The scholar in me resists simple comparisons between today's pandemic and Thucydides' account of the Athenian epidemic, but we have all experienced enough in recent months to read Thucydides with fresh eyes.

Two weeks into the outbreak of the pandemic in the Northeast, I (like everyone else) was beginning to learn to accept the new regimen and the upending of my calendar. Looking back I laugh at that conceit, the self-deception of calendar making, as though the calendar was ever mine to control, our plans ever not radically contingent on the lives of others and outside events. I was not so philosophical when the phone woke me past midnight on March 27. I wished it un-rung. Two weeks earlier a Delphic text message had startled my brother and me: "Dad is dead"—just like that. In the absence of a pronoun, my brother and I inferred the dad to be *our* father, and we panicked. But it turned out to be the sender's father and, recomposed, we sent commiserations.

Now, listening to the phone ring, some second sense told me that the oblique text had been prodromal. Then I heard it: my father was dead. As my mind unspooled before gathering itself again, I tried to piece together the how. The description I heard could have been symptoms of COVID-19—but we cannot know, given the lack of testing and my father's preexisting conditions. I offered blurred condolences to my father's second wife and son, whom I have never met, but whose voices I know well. "Please come," they said.

But I couldn't. Flight restrictions, I explained, meant that we would not be able to travel to Kenya for the funeral. I slept and then woke to news reports that police were firing tear gas to disperse the crowds at the Likoni ferry—the route that the ambulance would have to travel to take the body to the mortuary. And I found myself fretting about safe passage, not between this world and the next, but the earthly journey of twenty miles to find a temporary resting place for my father.

We worked together as a makeshift family to cobble together a funeral. My brother and I did what we could. On the other side of the world, eleven hours ahead of me, my brother edited our father's life for an obituary. Meanwhile I cut and pasted segments of the Anglican liturgy for the burial of the dead, choosing the psalms I thought would have meant the most to my father. And then the vigil, staying awake and holding my own ceremony in the hollow of morning to keep time with a funeral eight thousand miles away and seven hours ahead. I remembered my mother, thirty years ago, having heard too late of her own father's death in another country, sitting at the bottom of the garden weeping out of time.

I have learned lessons in remote mourning—how we remember the dead when they die far away from us. Thucydides gives short shrift to religiosity and too-easy credence in divine causation and its signs. He tells us that, in the context of the plague, people recalled an oracular verse from oral tradition predicting "a Dorian war will come, and with it plague," but that there was some dispute about whether the verse said *loimos* (plague) or *limos* (famine). "Under the circumstances," he remarks, "the opinion naturally prevailed that plague was mentioned; men shaped their memories in accordance with what they experienced. And yet, I suppose, if another Dorian war breaks out after this one, and it happens there is famine, they will probably recite accordingly." This passage came back to me as a cautionary tale about the ethics of memory as we struggle to do justice to the wide horizons of a life, and as a thought experiment about how we will choose to recall these times of widespread suffering.

My father's former students wrote and stirred dormant memories; these came to us on the winged words of social media. In the absence of present mourning, my brother and I relied more than ever on such memories, loaned from others, as confirmation that our father had lived in the world. One particular message woke me out of my private grief: reading it I became a girl of twelve or thirteen again, in our home on the campus where my father—a schoolteacher—was head of pastoral life during another plague, that of HIV/AIDS. Sitting in my bedroom at the front of the house, I watch a scene on a loop: students coming up the drive with the gait of those who are expectant but unsure of what to expect. I imagine the slow relay: a death from the virus, then a telegram for the attention of my father, then a message passed to a student in her dormitory, and her slow walk across campus, weaving in and out of shadow and light. The hushed tones as my father walked with her on the driveway and the brave line of the shoulders slowly crumbling and my father, who could be austere, crumbling with them. And sometimes, if a student could not stand, they would both sit on the wall outside my window, their slumped backs to me. Meanwhile my mother hovered in the doorway, ready to offer comfort. On the cusp of the 1990s these telegrams became more frequent as the virus that could not be named swept through families, taking parents before their time. Now, in this message from one of these former students, the arm that I saw reach out to comfort others comes back to me—and with it a reminder of the long arc of the global epidemic of HIV/AIDS that is still with us and a palpable sense of pandemic loss.

This was before the killing of George Floyd, a result of what Benjamin Crump, the Floyd family's attorney, described in *The Guardian* as "that other pandemic that we're far too familiar with in America, that pandemic of racism and discrimination." Thucydides' account of the plague cemented the tradition in classical political thought of disease in the city and the citizen body as a metaphor for social and political decay. The protests and other forms of direct political action in response to the killing of George Floyd, Breonna Taylor, Ahmaud Arbery, and "an untold number" of Black Americans are pressing this logic home and demanding a deeper diagnosis of what ails us.

What began as a national discourse about a strange new virus and a global pandemic has become a question about the stricken body of American democracy. In 1957 Richard Wright wrote, "The History of the Negro in America is the history of America written in vivid and bloody terms. . . . The Negro is America's metaphor." Are we ready to recognize, finally, that the Black body, Black life, and Black personhood are synecdoche for the Republic? In the midst of this pandemic we crave that most ambitious of cures—the cure of the ailing body politic.

Thucydides manages to hold his prose together, but I imagine that as he composed the plague narrative he was haunted by scenes of suffering and death, and that he remembered the citizen body of Athens falling apart and the swaggering heights from which it fell. As he reflected on the catastrophe of the plague, he may have remembered Sophocles' tragedy *Antigone,* performed in Athens before the plague in 442 or 441 BCE, in which the chorus sings a double-edged praise of human ingenuity—the "Ode to Man": "Many things are formidable and none more formidable than humankind," in Hugh Lloyd-Jones's translation. Sophocles' chorus proceeds to recite a catalogue of the skills of "all-resourceful" man, who "meets nothing in the future without resource," and has "contrived escape from incurable diseases." The tragic irony of this description seems to echo behind Thucydides' observation that "doctors had no effect . . . nor did any other human agency."

For his part, Thucydides offers the following explanation for his narrative of the plague: "I will say what it was like in its course and describe here, as one who had the plague myself and saw others suffering from it myself, the symptoms by which anyone who studies it cannot possibly fail to recognize it with this foreknowledge, if it ever strikes again." In other words, Thucydides describes the plague for his readers not as any kind of inoculation against the recurrence of the disease, but so that next time people will be wiser. We all know how that goes.

Safe

Elisa Gabbert

One weekend last August I rented a condo in Carbondale, Colorado, a mountain town a few hours west of Denver by car, to meet my parents for a mini-vacation. My husband and I left the city around midday on Friday, hoping to beat the traffic on I-70. My parents, who had a longer trip—coming up from El Paso, Texas, through Durango—expected to arrive by early evening. When we got to the house I texted my mom, and then I texted again after we got settled, to say we were walking to the main street, and asking her to let me know when they were close.

John and I wandered the length of the street, which was crowded with locals and tourists. It was still sunny outside. We went into an Italian restaurant and sat at the bar. I checked my phone frequently as we drank our wine. My parents were later than expected, and my mom still hadn't texted back. I stepped outside and tried to call her, then my dad; neither answered. I texted them both. *Is everything ok?* I looked at our text history and realized I hadn't heard from either of them in over two hours.

It's hard to overstate how uncharacteristic this was. My parents are road trip people; my father always drives, and my mother provides frequent status updates via text. They wouldn't travel without a car charger. Maybe she put her phone away and can't hear it, John suggested. This was so implausible it was impossible. My mother is a worrier too, and she would have been checking to make sure we had arrived safely.

The minutes passed; I finished my drink. I tried calling them again. I texted my brother to see if he had heard from them. John kept telling me not to panic; he was sure there was a reasonable explanation. To my mind, the reasonable explanation was that my parents had been in an accident on some vertiginous two-lane road and were trapped in the mangled vehicle. What should I even do? Call hospitals, the police? Involuntarily I began having anti-fantasies about my new life in grief. I imagined calling my manager to ask for some time off from work, and started crying. I was 70 percent sure they were dead.

Finally, finally, my mother called, wild with apologies. They had been crawling along in a construction zone, with no cell reception. She knew how worried I would be. She said she had kept her thumb on her phone continuously, waiting for a blip of a bar so she could send me a message. I cried again, harder now, with relief. Within twenty minutes they arrived, and we hugged. Their bodies were warm from the car. Later we went back to the Italian place for dinner and crowded around an outdoor table that barely had room for all our dishes and glasses of wine. The occasion felt particularly celebratory. "I'm so glad you're alive," I kept saying.

I woke up the next day feeling lazy and happy, my gratitude lingering like a buzz. Then I looked at my phone. There had just been a mass shooting at a Walmart in El Paso—my hometown, where my parents still live. I didn't have to be scared for them, since they were safe here, with us. Still, we were shocked. All morning John and I kept checking the news. As always, the number of casualties was initially unclear. The death toll would eventually amount to twenty-three; the shooting, which the *New York Times* would call "the deadliest attack to target Latinos in modern American history," is among the top ten deadliest mass shootings in the United States since 1949 (four of them occurred in Texas). We don't usually talk about things like gun control with my parents—our politics differ—but this event was literally close to home. We tested the edges of argument. Might it not alter their point of view? Wasn't it now personal? They didn't quite seem to think so. The store was nowhere near their house.

There was tension in the air, but we carried on with our plans. We drove to a nearby nature reserve where my mom could look at birds through her binoculars. When John and I got bored, we wandered away to a nearby street fair; he bought and devoured a peeled mango impaled on a wooden stick. That night we grilled steaks and drank several bottles of wine.

On Sunday morning I tried to read on the porch, but my mother came out to sit with me and kept wanting to talk. She's gregarious. I knew I wouldn't see her again until Christmas; I usually see her only twice a year. (For how many more years?) I should have cherished her company. But I'm sure I said, "Mom. I'm trying to read." I can hear myself saying it. For the remainder of the weekend I felt the normal amount of annoyance with my parents, and the normal amount of affection for them. I had gone right back to taking their existence for granted.

SINCE EARLY MARCH, when the country began to shut down in various degrees, I've often thought about how much of "normal life" I took for granted. If I needed something, or simply wanted it, I could just go and get it. I had never appreciated that my routines, in my largely white and middle-class neighborhood, weren't dangerous. I know this thought is not original—in fact it strikes me as profoundly unoriginal. In fact it seems like most people I know have been having all the same feelings in the same order. First I feared my parents wouldn't take the risk of the virus seriously enough. I started talking to them almost every day—pressuring my father, an internist, to close his office—then, after a few weeks, we spoke a little less often, having run out of things to say. Nothing new was happening. I watched a movie on my laptop, hyperaware of how often the characters touched their own faces. I had an anxiety dream that I'd forgotten about social distancing and accidentally gone to a party. I had a wish-fulfillment dream about grocery shopping, filling my cart with specialty meats and good olives at the deli. I went on a walk and felt like I was playing a live-action video game, trying to stay six feet away from other walkers and joggers at all times, while also trying not to get hit by a car. When I told my friends these things, or shared any recent observation or impression, they always said, *Me too!* or *Exact same.* We were all struggling to focus on reading and on work—our mostly inessential work, which we were still allowed to do, on the internet at home. We were having the same dreams.

Over the course of the first month, I read for longer and longer stretches, as though building my strength back up after an injury. When I couldn't read and wasn't working or sleeping, I chain-smoked crosswords, a kind of verbal solitaire that made a decent substitute for human conversation. One night I read for hours (*Rebecca,* by Daphne du Maurier—it helped that it was both suspenseful and a little silly) without looking at my phone. By mid-April I felt that my reading comprehension and concentration were back to normal. I spent an afternoon with a new book of poetry and made notes for a review—a peaceful reprieve. When I called my best friend, who lives in Brooklyn with her husband and toddler, she too was feeling better; she'd reached a plane of acceptance. We'd developed new routines; we had to admit we were lucky. Same feelings, same order. It's as if our interior lives that once felt so variegated, so individual, were just the result of having slightly different experiences at different times.

Not too long after this, I saw a CNN graphic that put the current U.S. death count from COVID-19 at more than forty thousand. The number was specific, not a rounded figure—a string of five non-zero digits. One of them was 7. The number blanked my mind. It felt unprocessable. These were verified deaths, in actual reality, but I could not imagine them—as though the size of the number, paradoxically, made each singular death less real. That number, as I write this, has more than doubled.

There's a passage from Barbara Tuchman's historical account of the fourteenth century, *A Distant Mirror*, that I've seen cited many times in the past six weeks:

> What was the human condition after the plague? Exhausted by deaths and sorrows and the morbid excesses of fear and hate, it ought to have shown some profound effects, but no radical change was immediately visible. The persistence of the normal is strong.

I know the passage well. I've written about it before, and that line about "the persistence of the normal" often comes to me in full; for a fraction of a second I mistake it for my own thought. The Black Death was interpreted as a punishment for sin and yet, Tuchman writes, the period after the plague ravaged Europe—somewhere between one-third and one-half of its occupants died—was if anything more disordered and immoral. The sinners who survived did not change their ways. The world collapsed around them and they moved on.

ONE EVENING IN APRIL my mother sends me a video she has recorded on her phone while walking slowly through her garden—all the roses are in bloom, pink roses, looking wild and overgrown. I can hear birds chirping in the video. My mother has birdbaths and bird-feeders all around her garden so she can bird-watch from the kitchen window or the back porch. The video makes me cry; it's so calming and beautiful.

Later I send her a package of shatterproof outdoor string lights as a Mother's Day present. The next weekend my father helps her hang them, and she sends me photos from her phone, taken at dusk, to show off their warm, inviting glow. In the second photo, which she's taken from the patio, I can see, through the mesh screen, the fuzzy outline of my father sitting inside on the porch. I cry again. These tears arrive suddenly, without warning—huge teardrops, like a child's, spill over and run down my cheeks. I am not even sad, exactly, just overwhelmed with feeling—with love, and relief that my parents are still safe, and that they have this flowering sanctuary, and yes, I guess sadness, that their haven is out of my reach.

I Can't Sleep

Emily Bernard

It's 1 a.m. I lie in my bed in the dark, my heart beating fast. I knew this would be a hard night; I got to bed by midnight, but the interior stream of words never stopped. I took drugs—both pharmaceutical and herbal (this is Vermont)—hoping they would quiet the flow and allow me to sleep. They didn't work; the stream rushed into a river. Phrases and sentences propel me upright. I turn on the light and scribble them quickly in a notebook, trying not to wake John, my husband, who sleeps soundly beside me.

I turn the light back off. Can I sleep now? I plead with the darkness. No. I drag myself out of bed and down two flights of stairs to the guest bedroom. I am afraid to be alone with my thoughts, but desperation overwhelms my fear. I take my iPad with me; it's less populated with social media platforms than my phone. I can't find the app for the flashlight. I keep tapping on my iPad to keep the light going on the screen. Tap, tap, tap.

My ankles hurt; I limp down the stairs, leaning on the banister. It may be general stiffness or something more serious, like plantar fasciitis, but I'm too afraid to go to my doctor right now. I received an email about the office's social-distancing protocols, but I allowed it to be swept away with the deluge of other information saturating my inbox. I turn on the light in the downstairs bathroom and stare in the mirror at my graying hair, untended by my hairdresser for more than three months. My twins are growing up and I feel myself growing old. The childlike joy that writing used to awaken in me is gone, replaced by a dull nothing. I am not writing out of pleasure; I am writing like a robot, fighting to be counted as human.

Drip, drip, drip. The words won't stop. It is 2:30 a.m. More notes. I put down the notebook I keep on the side table and tap on my iPad, raising it from sleep. Maybe the color and vibrancy of a movie or a television show will cheer me up. I scroll through the offerings. So many dramas about violence against men and women, Black death and female agony. I remember that a new episode of my favorite show, *Insecure,* is available on one of my streaming services. A portrait of Black life in Los Angeles, its first seasons included subplots about its characters' confrontations with white supremacy. But the current season features only nonwhite characters. They are beautiful and young, Black and Asian, gay and straight. My throat tightens as I watch the characters moving on the city streets, free of fears of contagion, of police violence. Simply living human lives in before times. There is a lot of talk about food, and several scenes involving sumptuous dishes (crispy squash flowers, garlic prawns, rib eye steak). I realize that I am hungry, but I'm too tired to go upstairs to the kitchen. More than food, anyway, I am hungry for those city streets of L.A. and other streets just like them in Brooklyn, New Haven, and Nashville, places where I feel free and that at various times in my life I have called home. In my neighborhood in Vermont, I am Black, female, and alone.

After the episode is over, I toss and turn. It's 3:30. Only two hours, I decide, before I can get out of bed without feeling like I've given up. The sun will have risen, bringing with it a sense of hope. I resist tuning into any newsfeeds on my iPad; I don't want to start the day feeling haunted by another person's death by way of the virus or the police.

My house is full of people and pets, but I am just as alone inside as I am outside in the streets of my neighborhood. I am trapped in language, a ceaseless ongoing monologue. I am trapped in unpleasant thoughts and memories. I have just read a book about white supremacy that made a convincing argument about the transhistorical continuity of racism as a fundamentally, irreversibly American phenomenon. I am starting to examine some of my memories in a new light. A recent interaction with a sour neighbor—an older white man—takes on a racial valence. I had convinced myself that the encounter was meaningless and had nothing to do with race. Now I decide that I was kidding myself. The conviction settles in along with the usual fear accompanying the realization that things between me and the sour neighbor could have escalated in the same way similar encounters unfold in this country and then appear in the news. I don't have to pass by his house again, I tell myself. I have nothing to prove, and I must focus on my safety. COVID-19 has limited the orbit of my life. A paralyzing awareness of my utter vulnerability to racist violence circumscribes my world even further.

I will tell John about the neighbor. I will instruct my children not to pass by his house on their walks with our dog. Except for the chore of dog walking, my daughters stay mostly inside with their parents. After all of these weeks at home, the usual boundaries between us have eroded. Now that they don't go to school, they can observe how I move through the day. My manner of working puzzles my daughter Giulia.

A few weeks ago, she came into my room when I was sitting in bed, reading a book. "I don't understand how you even have a career," she said. "I never see you working."

"Reading is work," I insisted.

She shook her head and left the room.

Giulia knows me better than anyone else, even better than my husband or her twin sister, Isabella. She knew that I was hiding my phone under the covers. I read my book in between scrolling through articles and posts about Black death and protests against police violence; in between the scrolling, I read my book. I wish I could disappear into books the way I always did in the before. I couldn't go back to willful ignorance if I tried. No more sleeping.

THE TERM *white supremacy* is now part of Isabella's everyday idiom. More than anyone else in our family, Isabella and I are both prisoners of our screens. She watched the videos of Black men being murdered by white men, even though I begged her not to. At fourteen my daughters have already experienced the painful effects of white supremacy. But I believe that innocence for them ended years ago, the precise moment being the morning after the 2016 presidential election.

White supremacy and Black death; #metoo and #blacklivesmatter. Karens. The current linguistic conceptual landscape is choking us, revealing us, reducing us. "Why do they hate us?" asks Isabella. She says she would like to ask a white supremacist this question. I love her faith in logic and humanity, but God forbid.

I love the home we have made of our house. I fell in love with its atmosphere the first moment I stepped through the door. Immediately I was facing a big bay window that looked out onto the woods whose tall trees continue to remind me of the endurance, order, and purity of nature. Haitian art decorated the walls of the foyer. A copy of *Citizen* by Claudia Rankine lay on top of the desk in one of the children's rooms. My realtor, whose name is Karen, told me that the wife was a doctor who directed a clean-water project in Haiti. Before she and her husband divorced, they were considering adopting a baby from Haiti. Karen knows what moves me. I decided on that first viewing that the house was meant for us.

Karen the realtor is the least Karen of all Karens. She is joyful, respectful, and intimate with me. The day she showed me the house, we sat in her pristine white Mercedes and confessed a mutual vanity about our hair. I miss her. I miss everyone. But all this missing is futile and only increases my global sense of despair. I must get better at being alone.

IT'S 4:15. I turn on the light. It is so quiet in here, but my fears are crowding me. My heart thuds. I think of the numbers of Black people who are dying, from COVID, from stress induced by racism. The sun is rising. I don't want to die. Not this way, not this day. Not anytime soon.

The light filters through the curtains: 5 a.m. Close enough. It's time to rise and face the day. I climb the stairs to the kitchen and turn on the kettle for my coffee. Our home is peaceful, our routines predictable. When John gets up, he will make his coffee in the other French press, the one I'm not allowed to use. I will join him in the kitchen. Maybe we will enjoy our typical race-related banter. When he and I rise at the same time, he makes my coffee exactly the way I want it. If he does it wrong, I correct him, and he tells me I am Blackwomansplaining him.

He keeps us safe, my husband. When I succumb to despair, too scared to leave our house, he keeps our home running. He tends to our public lives while I tend to our private lives, particularly the emotional lives of our children. I am the one they turn to with their fears and questions—about COVID, about racism, about whether one or the other will kill them. They love their father. We gather around the island in our kitchen and they pelt him with good-natured accusations of whitesplaining and mansplaining. An occasional #okay boomer. We transform terms meant to capture essential divisions between us into language that ultimately reinforces our common bond.

My coffee is ready. I return upstairs to my desk, in a room just off my bedroom. Moments after I turn on my computer, Giulia appears at my door, silent, holding Tom, one of our cats. The look in her eyes says that Tom found his way into her room and has been annoying her. She drops him to the floor and walks out. Everyone else is still in bed. I translate my notes into sentences fit for this essay. When I look at the clock, it is 8:40 a.m.

I check an app on my phone. Steady good weather today. The frank sunshine lights up my room and fills me with purpose. I am both awake and aware. It's not safe out there, but it is safe in here, on the island my husband and I created. Today I pledge to keep the treacherous water around us still and urge my daughters to focus on the sun.

Giving Up the Ghost

Hafizah Geter

It is his tenth birthday, and in South Carolina, my nephew Zayd sheds.

The roundness of his face slowly leaving. His innocence sloughing off. His jokes thrumming with the sophistication of a child who's learned life's plot twists from watching too much CNN.

In January my pregnant sister Jamila, her husband Alieu (a Gambian immigrant), and their two boys arrived at my father's house in Columbia from their current home in Beijing, my sister's belly eight months wide and ready to give birth to their third and final son. Then COVID-19 arrived. They found themselves trapped in America— my newest nephew, Ibraheema Alyaan, one of the many babies born into a world wearing the mark of a pandemic.

Jamila, Alieu, and my father—a visual artist—are news junkies. CNN, Rachel Maddow, and Joy Reid play for hours on a seldom-turned-off TV in my father's living room. Zayd can quote the president. He raises his small shoulders, two fingers from each hand thrown up in the air, his body giggling with satire as he confuses Nixon for 45. Zayd will quickly tell you that "Donald Trump doesn't like Black people." Even so, he's tired of living in Beijing, a country where so few boys look like him.

As the coronavirus death toll rises, as Black folks beg for testing, for treatment, for economic relief—for our pain to be believed—as my nephew watches my father convalesce from a February lung cancer diagnosis and a partial lobectomy, and as bodies flood the street to protest the lives murdered by police, I am reminded that there are a million ways to teach a Black boy about death. I know this country will try and strike down Zayd—still just a child, like Tamir Rice—the same way it does grown Black men.

Up and down my Brooklyn block, white chrysanthemums fling themselves open. In Ditmas Park, the trees have many lives. The eastern redbuds, magnolias, and Japanese cherry trees abandon their winter bareness for an explosion of white, pink, and purple flowers, their flowers then wilting away into bursts of glow green. In America, some of us die a thousand times. Our deaths tallied by views, by clicks, by how long it takes a doctor to believe you are sick, by the time it takes for the cop kneeling on your neck to be charged with murder.

Over FaceTime, my white partner Stephanie and I sing Zayd happy birthday. Nuh, four, giggles and tells us that today is going to be his birthday, too. Ibraheema, now four months old, sings to himself in the background. I can hear him smiling.

Today I woke up crying. I nipped it in the bud, wanting at least one day when grief doesn't blur joy. But I know what Black folks know: death can't be outwalked, outtalked from stalking you. George Floyd has been dead eight days and every picture or video I see is of a white cop kneeling on his neck. The cop's hand on his own hip, so casually it constructs a new kind of violence. Breonna Taylor has been dead for seventy-nine days and we are still begging America, *Say her name.* Tamir Rice would have been twenty, Trayvon twenty-five, the two of them strolling around with that swagger of Black boys whose mamas have finally deemed them grown enough for them to feel like men.

How does one give up the ghost?

The ghost, in this case, being the one a country makes of you.

I know, too, that though we lace our children with fear, we also flood them with possibility. We daisy-chain them in our lore. Our stories, like our love, are an unconfiscatable armor. I think of my great-grandma Lizzie nourishing households of poor Black folks from her Georgia garden, as if she were some kind of Jesus, with his two fish and five loaves of bread feeding the five thousand. I think of how in a single generation we've gone from sharecropping to college. All our miracles have a Black child's face.

A week after Zayd's birthday, Stephanie and I head to a neighborhood protest in Brooklyn. The abacus of Black death reminding us that George Floyd has been dead thirteen days.

Black body after Black body. Are we body or are we ghost?

Volunteers hand out face masks, gloves, and hand sanitizer. They offer cool water to the sea of protesters whose skin magnets the sun in the cordoned-off Brooklyn streets. Cops in bulletproof vests, without PPE, lean against buildings, licking their teeth like they're looking for a duel. Together, we demand life for every Black boy and girl, every Black woman, man, all our Black trans sisters and brothers. Together, we are chanting, *Fuck these racist-ass police! NYPD, suck my dick.* We embody a language of people who will not be refused our humanity. On any other day, this would get us killed. We are free and there is nothing the police can do about it, until they begin to do something about it. The cops, whispering, suddenly clump together, moving in angry-ant formation. I tell Stephanie, *It's time to go.* On the walk back, we don't comment on the helicopters we hear overhead. At home we open Twitter. We scan our feeds and see an officer swing a bicycle at someone like a bat. We see cops unsheathing their batons like swords, their weapons making hungry contact with bodies that brazenly demand life. The cops unleash pepper spray on protesters—a sea of skin, blood, and bone—bodies the state never intended to serve or protect.

IN THIS BODY, in this country, am I dead or am I living? Am I human or am I my country's ghost?

There are times I don't know. I peer back into my childhood: my father is painting in his art studio, my mother is on the phone with a cousin in Nigeria, her tongue clicking into a language I don't understand. I hear the cackle of my parents' laughter pouring from their Black bodies like warm rain on our hot '90s Akron summers. I see my childhood full of warnings, a childhood where to be Black is also a story of hands. Warnings not to touch anything in a store. Hands that keep themselves visible and flayed open on the street. Hands that know always to return empty lest I accidentally carry the danger America makes of me home.

I have three little Black and Muslim boys to love. Boys that a pandemic has trapped in the Confederate South. Boys who are Half-ricans just like me. We are the hunted living inside the haunt.

Lord, Allah, is my shadow my shadow?

Or is it the placeholder for the ghost America begs me to be?

IN THE COVID WORLD, stories are dying. A woman with a dead mother, this loss I know. How death becomes a vacancy of truth and narrative.

We have lost an astonishing amount of Holocaust survivors. *Poof,* and civil rights leaders disappear. The accountants of history, gone. The voices of people who did the best they could to balance a crooked country's scales. Larry Kramer, the activist who forced the nation to look at AIDS, dies and COVID prevents us from collectively mourning him, which means something in the world—something inside of us—dies twice.

I try to download my father's story as fast as I can. Knowing that the virus could take him, me—any one of us. Knowing that medical racism and an indifferent country ensures that this virus kills us at far higher rates than white people. COVID, the gap maker, the history breaker, the eraser. And yet I'm less afraid of COVID-19 than I am of being Black in America and needing help. It's not just a COVID death to contend with; it's the indignities of the way Black folks are left to die.

Black is a country and we have died in the cotton fields, both enslaved and free. Have died with our hands chemical-burned from the labor of cleaning white people's homes. We have died with our hands up. Have died while being refused our deaths, our waterlogged bodies raining over a child's casket. Our ghost stories populated with ancestors of all ages.

In South Carolina, my father puts garlic in the corners of his house to ward off the evil spirits that stalk the corners of his eyes. He draws my nephews in a charcoal series he's calling *Pandemic*. Here my father goes again, imagining us at the end of the world. In my father's ghost stories, Black folks always make it.

My father's voice bellows from inside my chest. My dead mother rides the wind around me—the kind of warm breeze that makes her grandson Nuh laugh, rubbing his belly in a way that cuts through time. Suddenly I can see Nuh there, in the future, the miracle of him as a much older man. And for a moment I forget that in our country "Black life" is the most dangerous dream—lest our freedom free all. They come for us knowing that we are freedom's imago. We, America's imaginal shape. Our freedom could make a new country.

We, the modern-day translation of the ancient Stoics.

The original Stoics believed that to experience true joy you should lean into death. They divided virtue into four types: wisdom, courage, temperance, and justice. Wisdom, in their view, was good sense and good calculation—the way we prepare Black children for the cops. Courage was one's ability to endure—like Black folks being forced to carry one humiliation after another. Temperance, one's access to self-control—the way we have yet to burn down this country. And justice is what we owe to one another—the way Black folks, despite a pandemic, protest in order to demand it for both our living and our dead. Zayd, Nuh, and Ibraheema are three Black boys inside the gun scope of a country. But still, despite the floods, I know that in South Carolina my father leans into laughter and my nephews dance below the sound like bells. Like any Black person, he is trying to stop America from turning our children into our ancestors. Our joy, our shield.

The Crisis of Asylum at Trump's Border Wall

Emily Gogolak

Driving south on 85 from a town called Why through the Organ Pipe Cactus National Monument, I was white-knuckling it. The pandemic had reduced traffic considerably in most parts of Arizona, but the narrow highway was clogged with dump trucks, most stamped with the words "Rock Solid Express" in blocky typeface and scrappy cursive. As they sped north, I saw that their trailers were full of earth that had been cleared to build a wall: *the* wall.

Rounding the next bend, I saw a valley in the distance with a dark line—maybe three miles off—running through it, too straight to be made by nature. It looked like someone had taken a fine-tip Sharpie to draw a line across the desert. It was May 20, five days after Arizona's reopening, and I was on a reporting trip to study the progress of Trump's border wall. The governor had issued a statewide stay-at-home order on March 31, but the pandemic hadn't stopped—or even slowed—work on the wall, to the distress of some residents.

The refusal to stop was hardly a surprise. Trump discusses the threat of the pandemic in language that mirrors the way he talks about migrants from Mexico and Central America, whose attempts to enter the United States he has repeatedly called an "invasion." "We will do everything in our power to keep the infection and those carrying the infection from entering our country," he said at a campaign rally in

Charleston early in the coronavirus outbreak. The wall itself is a stunning display of the administration's priorities: the country is ailing, record numbers of Americans are lining up at food banks, and meanwhile, on the southern border, an $11 billion altar to nativism keeps being built, beam by beam, to protect the homeland, even as it puts the workers building it at risk of catching the coronavirus.

Dust hazed up the sky. The hum of bulldozers grew louder the closer I got to the border. Such chaos felt antithetical to the landscape, a desert so pristine it looked unreal. Ocotillos, ironwoods, paloverdes, and the eponymous organ pipes—all still in bloom—offset the gray and reddish brown of the jagged hills above. I was headed out to the Quitobaquito Springs, an oasis that humans have been visiting for sixteen thousand years. The springs and this land are part of the O'odham homeland, which the Gadsden Purchase split up in 1854, when this border became the border.

I took a left just before Lukeville, Arizona, where Customs and Border Protection has an official port of entry for pedestrians and vehicles. The border had been closed to nonessential travel since March 21 and, aside from construction crews, it was nearly empty. This spot, halfway between Yuma and Tucson, is usually busy with Arizonans driving to the beaches in Puerto Peñasco. Worried I was misreading my National Park Service map, I pulled over and got out to ask a Border Patrol agent for directions. He told me I'd missed the right-hand turn for Quitobaquito on South Puerto Blanco Drive. He hopped out of the truck—buzz cut, glasses, no mask—and introduced himself as Jacob. He's forty-one and has been in the Border Patrol since he was twenty-six.

Before last August the wall didn't exist here; this part of the border was fortified by low-slung X-shaped barriers designed to stop vehicles from crossing. Now thirty-foot steel bollards—rust-colored poles, topped with flat metal panels to prevent climbing—extend from the port of entry in both directions. At the main crossing there's a small gap; to the west it climbs partway up a slope. There, where the construction has not yet begun, the border is demarcated simply by a thick line in the dirt. I asked Jacob what he made of it all. After some hesitation, he compared the wall to the Maginot Line, the fortifications that France built on its eastern border in the 1930s. In 1940 German troops went around the line, through Belgium. Now, he said, more migrants were crossing near the springs a dozen miles away, where the wall did not yet reach.

That Jacob sees the border through a military frame is telling. He is a veteran. "A year in combat rewires your brain," he told me, referring to his deployment to the Afghanistan-Pakistan border in 2004. Upon returning from infantry, he said, you are best qualified for three jobs: gym teacher, janitor, or cop. Veterans account for about 30 percent of Customs and Border Protection employees. As the historian Greg Grandin writes in *The End of the Myth: From the Frontier to the Border Wall in the Mind of America,* "Now the only thing endless is history's endless return, as veterans travel to the borderlands to rehearse how lost wars could have been won." I wondered why Jacob didn't become a cop in the Midwest, where he's from, and if the familiarity of a foreign desert had anything to do with it, but I didn't ask.

APART FROM THE WALL, the Sonoran Desert is itself a barrier between the United States and Mexico, between migrants and their relatives on the other side, between asylum seekers and refuge; it is a terrain hostile to human life. According to an online database of migrant deaths maintained by the Pima County Office of the Medical Examiner and the organization Humane Borders, more than three thousand bodies have been found in three counties in southern Arizona since 2000. This year alone so far, the skeletal remains of eleven migrants have been discovered in the Organ Pipe Cactus National Monument. None has been identified. Five were found just north of the springs.

Crucially, its dedication to building a physical barrier aside, the Trump administration has also constructed less visible—though perhaps even mightier—barriers to immigrants, like the one it spent the last three years raising around our asylum system; it has used the pandemic to build that barrier even higher.

The U.S. asylum system as we have known it was established forty springs ago. In 1980, with the passage of the Refugee Act, America adopted the international legal doctrine of non-refoulement, which states that the government cannot knowingly return a person "in any manner whatsoever" to a place where that person's life or liberty is at risk. Border Patrol agents are asylum's gatekeepers. Upon arresting migrants, an agent is required to inform them of their rights under U.S. law and to ask specific questions about why they left their home country and if they are afraid to return.

I SAID GOOD-BYE to Jacob and started off again for Quitobaquito. The road to the springs runs parallel to the wall, near Monument Hill, a burial ground for Apache warriors that is sacred to the O'odham. In February contractors made a series of controlled explosions on the hillside, loosening up hard rock and busting up little pockets of earth in order to lay a foundation for new stretches of wall. "For us, this is no different from DHS building a 30-foot wall along Arlington Cemetery or through the grounds of the National Cathedral," Ned Norris Jr., the chairman of the Tohono O'odham Nation, told a House subcommittee the same day that eighty-six explosives tore through the hill. Reporters were invited out to Lukeville to watch the blasts.

About seven miles from the springs, I turned around—the speeding trucks, blind curves, and rough road unnerved me. Back on 85 I drove due south toward the port of entry, passing signs reading VEHICLE AND PEDESTRIAN BARRIER REPLACEMENT PROJECT, rows of porta-potties and watercoolers, and modular housing for the wall builders, where social distancing must be a challenge. From this vantage, the wall is not an abstraction; it's built by workers sent out on a job, one the government has deemed "essential." A symbol is being concretized for the sake of voters who have never been to the borderlands. In mid-June the *New York Times* would report that two workers in southern Arizona, working on the wall in the Organ Pipe, tested positive for the virus, raising fears of an outbreak.

Near the camps squat organized stacks of steel bollards, waiting to be used. Lukeville itself is not quite a town—population thirty-five at last count—and there's little there: Gringo Pass Motel and RV Park, a gas station ("First Stop in the USA"), a convenience store, and a restaurant. If not for the pandemic, I'd hang out inside and talk to workers on break, but it's not safe enough to do that yet, so I just parked and watched. A few soldiers in fatigues strolled around the crossing, looking bored. (National Guard and active-duty troops have been deployed at ports along the border since 2018, when Trump raised hell about northbound caravans of Central American migrants.) A crane hovers precariously over the place where the physical wall ends. Contracts awarded to build this forty-three-mile section—which is supposed to be finished around Election Day, 2020—totaled $891 million. Trump apparently wants to paint the finished wall black. In an Arizona summer, black surfaces are hot to the touch.

I made a U-turn at the last place I could before crossing into Mexico. After a WELCOME TO ARIZONA sign, there's a National Parks Service sign: NATURAL AND CULTURAL RESOURCES ARE PROTECTED BY LAW. Just past the edge of the park, I reached the Border Patrol checkpoint. An agent asked where I live (Austin, but I've been quarantining in Phoenix), looked inside my car briefly, and encouraged me to come back to hike a particular canyon. In Why I turned onto Highway 86 and drove toward Tucson across Tohono O'odham Nation, where the poverty rate is nearly four times the national average. The Desert Diamond Casino had not yet reopened—a reminder of the slowness and stillness that governed life outside that remote construction site, which seemed to exist in a different, pre-pandemic world where people gathered and life moved fast.

Two ambulances and a huge flatbed hauling stacks of rusty metal something passed by. I realized they were border wall bollards. Another load passed in twenty minutes. Then another.

The Dancing Drum

Roger Reeves

"But the protest could not begin until the tambour was brought," said Chris.

Chris, a friend of mine who's quarantining in place with me after fleeing the ambulance siren–filled streets of Brooklyn during the pandemic, stands barefoot in my kitchen telling me about a protest in which he participated in Tegucigalpa after the coup d'état of President Manuel Zelaya in Honduras in 2009—a protest that couldn't begin until the tambour, a hand-carved drum, arrived and, with it, the music, dance, and marching of the protesters. As he talks, we periodically glance down at our phones. They beep and buzz with updates about the uprisings happening in Austin, Atlanta, Durham, Washington, DC, Minneapolis, Houston, Philadelphia, and Brooklyn, uprisings that began in response to Minneapolis police officer Derek Chauvin suffocating George Floyd, a Black man, to death. The fire, the smoke, the protests in Tegucigalpa are like the fire, smoke, and protests happening in America. In Honduras, it was the Garifuna—descendants of West African runaway slaves and Carib and Arawak Indians—protesting the Honduran military storming Zelaya's home at night, taking him from his bed, and putting him, still in his pajamas, on a military plane for Costa Rica. It was the Garifuna who helped to lead the protest in Tegucigalpa, because the post-coup

Honduran government targeted their lands for expropriation for tourism development (hotels) and agribusiness. In America it is the body of Black folks that must be conquered, expropriated, extracted from, and killed for the democracy to continue its experiment, an experiment languishing on gurneys in pandemic-filled hospitals. In fact, our pandemic-filled hospitals are another sign of the failing experiment, our failing democracy. It is as if beneath every presidential news conference—beneath each presidential dismissal of the seriousness of the pandemic and anti-Black racism in the country—R.E.M.'s "It's the End of the World as We Know It (And I Feel Fine)" is playing. Or the president is humming it in his head.

Chris and I discuss the overlaps of living in and through several apocalypses—the police and military rapaciously beating protesters and occupying the streets, the state-issued curfews, the small flights of fugitivity and pleasure that animate the days of a populace under lockdown.

But what brings us to talk about the tambour is the news of Black folks, here in America, dancing as they protest, on highways, in front of houses of state, while singing Frankie Beverly and Maze's "Before I Let Go." Here, as in Honduras, we, Black folks, must not only march but dance into catastrophe. Though it might seem strange, it is no accident in this recent round of protests in the United States that protesters brandish and deploy civil disobedience and joy in the face of tear gas, rubber bullets, dogs, and dour, helmeted police. As scholar Aliyyah I. Abdur-Rahman points out, "The future is yet to come and already past." In other words, if we wait for legislation, corporate benevolence, or some amorphous future, we might never experience the ecstasy we imagine, and that we know we deserve. So we must turn from the teleological, its notions of patient progress, and embrace the joy that allegedly lies on the other side of conquering struggle. Ecstasy now. I tell Chris about an essay I'm writing about this idea—ecstasy as a type of protest, that we might pinch our plea-sure in the middle of surveillance and sequestering, much like en-slaved Africans did while being surveilled by the masters during plantation dances.

Chris dips his head for a moment, falling into silence, one of those silences in which memory moves you out of one time and into another. He is back in Tegucigalpa. The tambour has finally arrived. He is telling all of this to me while looking out through the kitchen window into the darkness of the backyard—out, out into the past. The tambour is played, and the dancing begins. And the ritual smoke and the ritual bathing in smoke. Those who are not Garifuna join, invited in to be blessed and covered; however, they begin to make a mockery of the ritual, erotically dancing, gesticulating, and guffaw-ing over themselves.

Something similar is happening in America. During protests against anti-Blackness in Los Angeles, Atlanta, Newark, Durham, and Washington, DC, following the killing of George Floyd, demonstra-tors have juked, krumped, and danced while chanting, "No justice, no peace / Fuck these racist-ass police" in the middle of intersections. Calling for ecstasy now, Black folks luxuriantly revel in the aliveness of their bodies. In the flexed arm, in the arched back, in the hop and turn, we subvert the prevailing myth of the disposability of Black bodies. We ironize and wallow in the abjection of our surveillance. Holding up signs that read, "LET JUSTICE FLOW LIKE A RIVER," we enact an ecstatic present and future without the need for legislative or executive order. We are not waiting on some benign congress of politicians to grant us a future. We are granting it to ourselves in the form of embodied ecstasy.

And that ecstasy calls out to others, including, ironically, the Na-tional Guardsmen and police officers who stand by watching. They, too, want to shuffle and drop it low. And some do. As Hope Ford, a reporter for Channel 11 in Atlanta, noted in her broadcast on the night of June 4, once protesters started dancing at the corner of Centennial Park and Marietta, the National Guard members kept glancing toward their commanding officer, asking if they could dance. Finally the commanding officer gave his permission, and the soldiers joined in. They moved toward the joy they saw in the protesters. The National Guard's desire to dance exposes the irrepressible joy of being in one's body, the seduction of a freedom that is inhabited in spite of its possible impermanence. Quite simply, the body will always move toward ecstasy. Even if only for a moment. As Ford reported, after the dancing was over and time drew closer to curfew, the National Guard and the Atlanta police began expelling their former dance partners in an effort to clear the streets. Conflict arose. The space of joy was closed, and state-issued catastrophe was reinstituted.

I DON'T READ this short-lived moment of relational joy as a failure because the Georgia National Guard and the Atlanta police settled back into their state-issued instrumentality behind their batons and shields. What this moment ushers in is the notion that moments of relational joy can be opened up whenever and in front of whomever. It makes the possibility of ecstasy in the face of catastrophe *more* possible. As Sun Ra wrote in a poem originally published in *Esquire* in July 1969 to commemorate Neil Armstrong's moonwalk, when humanity achieves one impossibility, the chance of achieving another is more likely. These dancing demonstrators have touched the impossible, have made joy a possibility in the middle of catastrophe. Now this impossibility calls out to others. They call out to their kin: *Come out, come out, wherever you are.* And in doing so they make a tradition that hitherto did not exist. The make another pattern. A Black future. Liberation.

Notes and Sources

Cannon Fodder
Postscript, July 2020: My hospital now admits only a few new COVID-19 patients each day, whereas at peak we were caring for many hundreds at once. During New York City's spring surge of cases, "only" a few of my colleagues became gravely ill. Of the COVID-19 patients still in our hospital, the majority have or are recovering from tracheostomy collars, methods of ventilating a patient through a hole in the neck. Though grisly, these holes are stigmata of survival: marking out those patients who suffered illness long enough—and didn't die—that their doctors sought more durable ways of getting oxygen to their lungs, freeing their mouths up for the slow reinitiation of swallowing, speaking, eating. When my workdays run long, it's now in service to these finer points of recuperation. Meanwhile, emerging data make clear that people of color disproportionately suffered the pandemic's worst assaults. This summer of Black Lives Matter is a welcome revolt against still other forms of senseless death.

There's a Sickness Outside
Linda Nash, *Inescapable Ecologies: A History of Environment, Disease, and Knowledge* (Berkeley: University of California Press, 2006).

Medicine's Innovation Problem
Phil Galewitz, "Telemedicine Surges, Fueled by Coronavirus Fears and Shift in Payment Rules," *Kaiser Health News,* March 27, 2020, https://khn .org/news/telemedicine-surges-fueled-by-coronavirus-fears-and-shift -in-payment-rules/.

"Medicare Telemedicine Health Care Provider Fact Sheet," *Center for Medicare and Medicaid Services,* March 17, 2020, https://www.cms.gov/news room/fact-sheets/medicare-telemedicine-health-care-provider-fact -sheet.

"Order Expanding Access to Telehealth Services and to Protect Health Care Providers," Office of the Governor, Commonwealth of Massachusetts, March 15, 2020, https://www.mass.gov/doc/march-15-2020-telehealth -order/download.

Eric Wicklund, "Humana Adds Telehealth Coverage, Services to Address Coronavirus Pandemic," *mHealthIntelligence,* March 25, 2020, https:// mhealthintelligence.com/news/humana-adds-telehealth-coverage -services-to-address-coronavirus-pandemic.

"Waiver or Modification of Requirements under Section 1135 of the Social Security Act," U.S. Department of Health and Human Services, March 13, 2020, https://www.phe.gov/emergency/news/healthactions/section 1135/Pages/covid19-13March20.aspx.

The Law of *Salus Populi*

Marcus Tullius Cicero, *Cicero: On the Republic. On the Laws,* trans. Clinton W. Keyes (Suffolk, U.K.: Harvard University Press, 1928).

Leroy Parker and Robert H. Worthington, *The Law of Public Health and Safety and the Powers and Duties of Boards of Health* (Albany: Matthew Bender, 1892).

Charles E. Rosenberg, *The Cholera Years: The United States in 1832, 1849, and 1866* (Chicago: University of Chicago Press, 1962).

William J. Novak, *The People's Welfare: Law and Regulation in Nineteenth-Century America* (Chapel Hill: University of North Carolina Press, 1996).

W. P. Prentice, *Police Powers Arising under the Law of Overruling Necessity* (Albany: Banks and Brothers, 1894).

Amasa J. Parker, *Reports of Decisions in Criminal Cases Made at Term, at Chambers, and in the Courts of Oyer and Terminer of the State of New York* (Albany: W. C. Little, 1858).

"Jacobson v. Massachusetts," Oyez, accessed June 26, 2020, https://www
.oyez.org/cases/1900-1940/197us11.

Michael Willrich, *Pox: An American History* (New York: Penguin, 2011).

Jennifer Schuessler, "Liberation as Death Sentence," *New York Times,* June
10, 2012, https://www.nytimes.com/2012/06/11/books/sick-from-freedom
-by-jim-downs-about-freed-slaves.html.

Felice Batlan, "Law in the Time of Cholera: Disease, State Power, and Quarantines Past and Future," *Temple Law Review* 80 (2007): 53, https://
ssrn.com/abstract=1719144.

Nayan Shah, *Contagious Divides: Epidemics and Race in San Francisco's
Chinatown* (Berkeley: University of California Press, 2001).

Natalia Molina, *Fit to Be Citizens? Public Health and Race in Los Angeles,
1879–1939* (Berkeley: University of California Press, 2006).

Samuel Kelton Roberts Jr., *Infectious Fear: Politics, Disease, and the Health Effects
of Segregation* (Chapel Hill: University of North Carolina Press, 2009).

David France, *How to Survive a Plague: The Inside Story of How Citizens and
Science Tamed AIDS* (New York: Knopf, 2016).

Jan H. Richardus and Anton E. Kunst, "Black-White Differences in Infectious Disease Mortality in the United States," *American Journal of Public Health* 91, no. 8 (August 2001): 1251–1253, doi: 10.2105/ajph.91.8.1251.

Steve Vladeck (@steve_vladeck), "Just to be clear, @realDonaldTrump
STILL hasn't actually used the DPA," Twitter, March 27, 2020, 5:36
p.m., https://twitter.com/steve_vladeck/status/1243653231378661376.

Pandemic Inequality

Postscript, July 2020: When this essay was originally published on April 3,
2020, Brazil counted 9,216 COVID-19 cases and 365 deaths. On July
14, 2020, when it was revised, Brazil counted 75,366 deaths (the second
highest number in the world after the United States) and 1,966,748
infections. The most comprehensive study so far on the relationship between socioeconomic inequality and COVID-19, analyzing 29,993 cases
of infection (of which 13,558 resulted in death) confirms the negative
feedback loop effect: the lethality rate of COVID-19 in Brazil is three

times higher in individuals without formal education (71.3 percent) than in those with a university degree (22.5 percent). Moreover, Black and mixed-race people are 17 percent more likely to die of COVID-19 than white people (55 percent and 38 percent, respectively).

"UNAIDS Data 2019," UNAIDS.org, 2019, https://www.unaids.org/sites /default/files/media_asset/2019-UNAIDS-data_en.pdf.

Paul Denning and Elizabeth DiNenno, "Communities in Crisis: Is There a Generalized HIV Epidemic in Impoverished Urban Areas of the United States?" Center for Disease Control and Prevention, accessed June 28, 2020, https://www.cdc.gov/hiv/group/poverty.html.

Sandra Crouse Quinn and Supriya Kumar, "Health Inequalities and Infectious Disease Epidemics: A Challenge for Global Health Security," *Biosecurity and Bioterrorism: Biodefense Strategy, Practice, and Science* 12, no. 5 (September 2014): 263–273, https://doi.org/10.1089/bsp.2014.0032.

"Covid-19," MRC Centre for Global Infectious Disease Analysis, Imperial College London, accessed June 28, 2020, http://www.imperial.ac.uk /mrc-global-infectious-disease-analysis/covid-19/.

Ligia Guimáres, "Favelas Serão as Grandes Vítimas do Coronavírus no Brasil, diz Líder de Paraisópolis," *BBC News Brasil,* March 18, 2020, https:// www.bbc.com/portuguese/brasil-51954958.

Ravi Agrawal, "India's Lockdown Helps Its Rich but Ignores Its Poor," *Foreign Policy,* March 31, 2020, https://foreignpolicy.com/2020/03/31 /india-lockdown-helps-rich-ignores-poor-coronavirus-public-health/.

Charlotte Graham-McLay, "New Zealand Launches Massive Spending Package to Combat COVID-19," *The Guardian,* March 17, 2020, https:// www.theguardian.com/world/2020/mar/17/new-zealand-launches -massive-spending-package-to-combat-covid-19.

Sirenland

"Will you / Hug me through the phone": Lyrics by Sandy Placido. Reprinted by permission.

The White String

Etel Adnan, *Time,* trans. Sarah Riggs (Brooklyn: Nightboat Books, 2019). Selections reprinted by permission of *Time.*

Welcome to Zoom University

Manny Fernandez and David Montgomery, "Texas Tries to Balance Local Control with the Threat of a Pandemic," *New York Times,* March 25, 2020, https://www.nytimes.com/2020/03/24/us/coronavirus-texas-patrick -abbott.html.

"Fast Facts: Distance Learning," National Center for Education Statistics, accessed June 29, 2020, https://nces.ed.gov/fastfacts/display.asp?id=80.

Reading *The Decameron* through the Lens of COVID-19

All translations are from Giovanni Boccaccio, *The Decameron,* trans. Wayne A. Rebhorn (New York: Norton, 2013).

Lauren Gambino, " 'We're on the Other Side of the Mountain': Cuomo Hails Falling Rate of Coronavirus Infections," *The Guardian,* May 11, 2020, https://www.theguardian.com/us-news/2020/may/11/new-york -coronavirus-rate-infections-cuomo-hails-progress.

Dan Barry, "Optimism Is Less Distant as Global Coronavirus Battle Rages On," *New York Times,* April 8, 2020, https://www.nytimes.com/2020/04/08 /us/coronavirus-global-progress.html?auth=login-email&login=email.

A Commencement Deferred

Yiyun Li, "To Speak Is to Blunder," *The New Yorker,* January 2, 2017, https:// www.newyorker.com/magazine/2017/01/02/to-speak-is-to-blunder.

History Is Another Word for Trauma

Selections from the unpublished letters of Cynthia Erskine to Rachel Jami- son Webster reprinted with permission by Rachel Jamison Webster.

The Children Know

John Ashbery, "How to Continue," in *Notes from the Air: Selected Later Poems* (New York: Ecco, 2007), 117–118.

Get the Shovel

"CJLS Guidance for Remote Minyanim in a Time of COVID-19," The Rabbinical Assembly, March 17, 2020, http://www.rabbinicalassembly .org/story/cjls-guidance-remote-minyanim-time-covid-19.

Mary Meisenzhal, "This Is What Getting Married over Zoom Is Like, According to 2 Couples Who Had to Change Their Wedding Plans Due to the Coronavirus," *Business Insider,* April 23, 2020, https://www.business insider.com/zoom-weddings-during-coronavirus-photos-2020-4.

"NYC Funeral Home Stored Dozens of Bodies in U-Haul Trucks, Producing 'Overwhelming' Stench," *CBS News,* April 30, 2020, https://www .cbsnews.com/news/bodies-u-haul-trucks-new-york-funeral-home -covid-19/.

Kirk Johnson, "Coronavirus Means Funerals Must Wait: 'We Can't Properly Bury Our Dead,'" *New York Times,* March 26, 2020, http://www .nytimes.com/2020/03/25/us/coronavirus-funerals.html.

Christopher Stoney et al., "Steadily Increasing Control: The Professionalization of Mass Death," *Journal of Contingencies and Crisis Management* 19, no. 2. (2011), https://doi.org/10.1111/j.1468-5973.2011.00635.x.

Jacqueline A. Merrill et al., "Are We Ready for Mass Fatality Incidents? Preparedness of the US Mass Fatality Infrastructure," *Disaster Medicine and Public Health Preparedness* 10, no. 1 (2015): 87–97, https://doi.org /10.1017/dmp.2015.135.

Doris Gutsmiedl-Schümann et al., "Digging Up the Plague: A Diachronic Comparison of aDNA Confirmed Plague Burials and Associated Burial Customs in Germany," *Praehistorische Zeitschrift* 92, no. 2 (2017), https:// doi.org/10.1515/pz-2017-0018.

Meg Anderson, "Burials on New York Island Are Not New, but Are Increasing during Pandemic," *National Public Radio,* April 10, 2020, https:// www.npr.org/sections/coronavirus-live-updates/2020/04/10/831875297 /burials-on-new-york-island-are-not-new-but-are-increasing-during -pandemic.

Jacob Riis, Collected Photographs, Museum of the City of New York, accessed June 4, 2020, https://collections.mcny.org/CS.aspx?VP3=Search Result&VBID=24UP1GMH39YOH&SMLS=1&RW=1922&RH=1031 &VP3=SearchResult&VBID=24UP1GMH39YOH&SMLS=1&RW =1922&RH=1031.

Corey Kilgannon, "Dead of AIDS and Forgotten in Potter's Field," *New*

York Times, July 3, 2018, http://www.nytimes.com/2018/07/03/nyregion /hart-island-aids-new-york.html.

Ryan Grim, "Rikers Island Inmates Offered PPE and $6 an Hour to Dig Mass Graves," *The Intercept,* March 31, 2020, https://theintercept.com /2020/03/31/rikers-island-coronavirus-mass-graves/.

Asher Stockler, "More Than 700 People Have Tested Positive for Coronavirus on Rikers Island, Including Over 440 Staff," *Newsweek,* April 8, 2020, http://www.newsweek.com/rikers-island-covid-19-new-york-city -1496872.

Nina Bernstein, "Bodies Given to N.Y.U. Ended Up in Mass Graves, Despite Donors' Wishes," *New York Times,* May 27, 2016, http://www .nytimes.com/2016/05/28/nyregion/bodies-given-to-nyu-ended-up-in -mass-graves-despite-donors-wishes.html.

"Identifying Missing Persons and Unidentified Decedents," National Institute of Justice, February 26, 2012, https://nij.ojp.gov/topics/articles /identifying-missing-persons-and-unidentified-decedents.

Liv Nilsson Stutz and Sarah Tarlow, eds., *The Oxford Handbook of the Archaeology of Death and Burial* (Oxford: Oxford University Press, 2013).

Maurice Bloch and Jonathan Parry, eds., *Death and the Regeneration of Life* (Cambridge: Cambridge University Press, 1982).

Inger Agger, "Calming the Mind: Healing After Mass Atrocity in Cambodia," *Transcultural Psychiatry* 52, no. 4, (2015): 543–60, 10.1177 /1363461514568336.

Louis FitzGibbon, *Unpitied and Unknown* (London: Bachman and Turner, 1975).

Carrie Jung, "Laid to Rest: A Proper Burial for the Poor," *National Public Radio,* August 8, 2013, http://www.npr.org/2013/08/08/209873419/laid -to-rest-a-proper-burial-for-the-poor.

The Jail Crisis

Ross MacDonald MD, "A message from the Chief Physician of Rikers Island for the judges and prosecutors of New York: We who care for those you detain noticed how swiftly you closed your courts in response to

#COVID19." From the twitter feed of Dr. Ross MacDonald, Chief Physician of New York City's Correctional Health Services, March 18, 2020, https://twitter.com/RossMacDonaldMD/status/1240455796946800641. The Legal Aid Society, "COVID-19 Infection Tracking: Data Archive," last updated May 15, 2020, https://legalaidnyc.org/covid-19-infection-tracking -in-nyc-jails/data-archive/.

Coronavirus and the Danger of Disbelief

Joshua Lederberg, Robert E. Shope, and Stanley C. Oaks Jr., eds., *Emerging Infections: Microbial Threats to Health in the United States* (Washington, DC: National Academy Press, 1992), https://www.nap.edu/read/2008 /chapter/1.

Dan Diamond, "Inside America's 2-Decade Failure to Prepare for Coronavirus," *Politico*, April 11, 2020, https://www.politico.com/news/magazine /2020/04/11/america-two-decade-failure-prepare-coronavirus-179574.

"Playbook for Early Response to High-Consequence Emerging Infectious Disease Threats and Biological Incidents," https://assets.documentcloud .org/documents/6819268/Pandemic-Playbook.pdf.

William James, "The Moral Philosopher and the Moral Life," in *William James: Essays and Lectures,* ed. Richard Kamber and Daniel Kolak (London: Routledge 2007), 245.

William James, "The Perception of Reality," in *Complete Works of William James* (East Sussex, U.K.: Delphi Classics, 2018).

Anna Freud, *The Ego and the Mechanisms of Defense* (London: Hogarth and the Institute of Psychoanalysis, 1937).

John Barry, "What the 1918 Flu Pandemic Can Tell Us about the COVID-19 Crisis," interview by Terry Gross, *Fresh Air,* NPR, May 14, 2020, audio, 25:46, https://www.npr.org/2020/05/14/855986938/what-the-1918 -flu-pandemic-can-tell-us-about-the-covid-19-crisis.

Invisible Kingdoms

"Cynthia Ozick Reads Steven Millhauser," December 17, 2010, in *The New Yorker: Fiction,* produced by *The New Yorker* and *WNYC,* podcast, MP3

audio, 36:54, https://podcasts.apple.com/cr/podcast/cynthia-ozick-reads
-steven-millhauser/id256945396?i=1000373199600&l=en.

Charles Yu, "The Pre-Pandemic Universe Was the Fiction," *The Atlantic,*
April 15, 2020, https://www.theatlantic.com/culture/archive/2020/04
/charles-yu-science-fiction-reality-life-pandemic/609985/.

Charles Creitz, "St. John's Church Rector on Aftermath of Fire, Impromptu
Trump Visit: 'Like I'm in Some Alternative Universe,'" *Fox News,* June 1,
2020, https://www.foxnews.com/media/st-johns-rector-fire-impromptu
-trump-visit.

Dan Zak et al., "'This Can't Be Happening': An Oral History of 48 Surreal,
Violent, Biblical Minutes in Washington," *Washington Post,* June 2, 2020,
https://www.washingtonpost.com/lifestyle/style/this-cant-be-happening
-an-oral-history-of-48-surreal-violent-biblical-minutes-in-washington
/2020/06/02/6683d36e-a4e3-11ea-b619-3f9133bbb482_story.html.

Caio Barretto Briso and Tom Phillips, "Coronavirus Parties Highlight Brazil's Fractured Approach to Pandemic," *The Guardian,* June 9, 2020,
https://www.theguardian.com/world/2020/jun/09/brazil-coronavirus
-parties.

Lives or Livelihoods

Jeffrey Moyo and Rick Gladstone, "'We'd Prefer the Food': Zimbabwe Fears
a Famine Is in Its Future," *New York Times,* December 25, 2019, https://
www.nytimes.com/2019/12/25/world/africa/zimbabwe-hunger-famine
.html.

"Zimbabwe: Unsafe Water Raises COVID-19 Risks," Human Rights Watch,
April 15, 2020, https://www.hrw.org/news/2020/04/15/zimbabwe-unsafe
-water-raises-covid-19-risks#.

Thucydides in Times of Trouble

All quotes from Thucydides' *History* are taken from Steven Lattimore's translation: Thucydides, *The Peloponnesian War,* trans. Steven Lattimore (In-
dianapolis: Hackett, 1998).

Hippocrates, *Ancient Medicine: Airs, Waters, Places: Epidemics 1 and 3; The*

Oath, Precepts, Nutriment, trans. W. H. S. Jones, Loeb Classical Library 147 (Cambridge: Harvard University Press 1923).

For a helpful discussion of Thucydides' engagement with contemporary Hippocratic medicine, see Rosalind Thomas, "Thucydides' Intellectual Milieu and the Plague," in *Brill's Companion to Thucydides,* ed. Antonios Rengakos and Antonis Tsakmakis (Leiden: Brill, 2006), 87–108.

The connection with Pericles' earlier speech on Athenian war strategy is made by June Allison in "Pericles' Policy and the Plague," *Historia* 32, no. 1 (1983): 14–23.

Rachel Bruzzone, "*Polemos, Pathemata,* and Plague: Thucydides' Narrative and the Tradition of Upheaval," *Greek, Roman, and Byzantine Studies* 57 (2017): 882–909.

Chris McGreal, "'Get Your Knee off Our Necks': Sharpton Delivers Moving Eulogy at Floyd Memorial," *The Guardian,* June 4, 2020, https://www.theguardian.com/us-news/2020/jun/04/george-floyd-memorial-minneapolis.

Richard Wright, "*White Man, Listen!*" [1957], in *Black Power: Three Books from Exile; "Black Power"; "The Color Curtain"; and "White Man, Listen!"* (New York: Harper Perennial, 2008), 630–812.

Sophocles, *Antigone,* in *Sophocles: "Antigone," "The Women of Trachis," "Philoctetes," "Oedipus at Colonus,"* trans. Hugh Lloyd-Jones. Loeb Classical Library 21 (Cambridge: Harvard University Press, 1994).

Safe

Nicholas Bogel-Burroughs, "'I'm the Shooter': El Paso Suspect Confessed to Targeting Mexicans, Police Say," *New York Times,* August 9, 2019, https://www.nytimes.com/2019/08/09/us/el-paso-suspect-confession.html.

Barbara W. Tuchman, *A Distant Mirror: The Calamitous 14th Century* (New York: Ballantine Books, 1978), 116.

The Crisis of Asylum at Trump's Border Wall

Curt Prendergast, "Democrats Call for Halt to Border Wall Construction during Coronavirus Pandemic," *Tucson.com,* April 27, 2020, https://

tucson.com/news/local/democrats-call-for-halt-to-border-wall-con
struction-during-coronavirus-pandemic/article_472eb647-9fdb-554d
-a5f0-9514f5d776fe.html.

Nick Miroff and Josh Dawsey, "Trump Order to Paint Border Wall Black
Could Drive Up Cost $500 Million or More," *Washington Post,* May
6, 2020, https://www.washingtonpost.com/immigration/trump-border
-wall-black-paint/2020/05/06/dbda8ae4-8eff-11ea-8df0-ee33c3f5b0d6
_story.html.

"Organ Pipe Cactus," National Park Service, accessed June 28, 2020, https://
www.nps.gov/orpi/learn/historyculture/quitobaquito-springs.htm.

"CBP Recognized as One of the Best Companies for Veterans by Monster.
com," U.S. Customs and Border Protection, November 5, 2018, https://
www.cbp.gov/newsroom/national-media-release/cbp-recognized-one
-best-companies-veterans-monstercom.

Greg Grandin, *The End of the Myth: From the Frontier to the Border Wall in
the Mind of America* (New York: Metropolitan Books, 2020).

"Arizona OpenGIS Initiative for Deceased Migrants," Humane Borders,
accessed June 28, 2020, https://humaneborders.info/app/map.asp.

"Southwest Border Migration FY 2020," U.S. Customs and Border Protection, last modified June 12, 2020, https://www.cbp.gov/newsroom/stats
/sw-border-migration.

Nick Miroff, "Under Coronavirus Immigration Measures, U.S. Is Expelling
Border-Crossers to Mexico in an Average of 96 Minutes," *Washington
Post,* March 30, 2020, https://www.washingtonpost.com/immigration
/coronavirus-immigration-border-96-minutes/2020/03/30/13af805c-72c5
-11ea-ae50-7148009252e3_story.html.

Emily Gogolak, "How Trump Moved the Mexican Border North," *Politico,*
April 13, 2018, https://www.politico.com/magazine/story/2018/04/13
/donald-trump-deportation-immigration-texas-217990.

Caitlin Dickerson, "10 Years Old, Tearful and Confused After a Sudden
Deportation," *New York Times,* May 21, 2020, https://www.nytimes
.com/2020/05/20/us/coronavirus-migrant-children-unaccompanied
-minors.html.

Rafael Carranza and Daniel Gonzalez, "Tohono O'odham Nation Chairman

Compares Border Blast to Desecration of Arlington National Cemetery," *AZ Central,* February 26, 2020, https://www.azcentral.com/story/news/politics/border-issues/2020/02/26/tribal-leader-compares-border-wall-blasting-ancestral-lands-akin-desecration-arlington-cemetery/4884258002/.

Ryan Deveraux, "The Border Patrol Invited the Press to Watch It Blow Up a National Monument," *The Intercept,* February 27, 2020, https://theintercept.com/2020/02/27/border-wall-construction-organ-pipe-explosion/.

Simon Romero, "Arizona Finds Coronavirus among Border Wall Workers," *New York Times,* June 12, 2020.

Zach Montague, "Pentagon to Send 2,100 More Troops to the Southwestern Border," *New York Times,* July 17, 2019, https://www.nytimes.com/2019/07/17/us/politics/troops-border-immigration.html.

"Arizona Crews Blast National Monument Hill for Border Wall," *AP News,* February 7, 2020, https://apnews.com/a49dd620056cfc83003eb3875cbf16ef.

"Tohono O'odham Nation Reservation," Census Reporter, accessed June 28, 2020, https://censusreporter.org/profiles/25200US4200R-tohono-oodham-nation-reservation/.

The Dancing Drum

Aliyyah I. Abdur-Rahman, "The Black Ecstatic," *GLQ: A Journal of Gay and Lesbian Studies* 24, nos. 2–3 (June 2018).

Acknowledgments

This book would not have been possible without the work of key members of the editorial team at *The Yale Review*. Special thanks are due to the *Review*'s editors, Andrew Heisel, Maggie Millner, Rachel Mannheimer, and Paul Franz, who first commissioned and edited many of these pieces; to Susan Bianconi, the *Review*'s associate editor, who kept the *Review* running even under the great challenge of remote operations; and our assistant editors, Brianna Elatove, Ted Hamilton, Bianca Ibarlucea, Spencer Lee-Lenfield, Jessica Marion Modi, and Maru Pabón, as well as our copy editor, Susan Laity (who also acted as our production editor at Yale University Press). James Surowiecki provided invaluable editorial advice. The *Review* and I benefited tremendously from the help of our inaugural class of undergraduate *Yale Review* fellows: Ali Brown, Oona Holahan, Charlie Lee, Sara Luzuriaga, Sean Lynch, Meghana Mysore, Liana van Nostrand, and Eric O'Keefe-Krebs.

And, of course, I must thank the contributors, each of whom worked hard with us on these pieces, in what was surely a triumph of will over often chaotic, and certainly challenging, circumstances. We are honored to work with all of you.

Finally, this book would not exist without the vision of its editor, Jennifer Banks, and John Donatich. Our deep thanks.

Contributors

NITIN AHUJA is an assistant professor of clinical medicine in the Division of Gastroenterology and Hepatology at the University of Pennsylvania.

EMILY BERNARD is the author of a new collection of essays, *Black Is the Body: Stories from My Grandmother's Time, My Mother's Time, and Mine.* She is the Julian Lindsay Green and Gold Professor of English at the University of Vermont.

VICTORIA CHANG's poetry books include *OBIT, Barbie Chang, The Boss, Salvinia Molesta,* and *Circle.* Her children's books include *Is Mommy?* illustrated by Marla Frazee, and *Love, Love,* a middle-grade novel. She lives in Los Angeles and is the program chair of Antioch's Low-Residency MFA Program.

ALICIA MIRELES CHRISTOFF is a Mexican American writer and associate professor of English at Amherst College. She is the author of *Novel Relations: Victorian Fiction and British Psychoanalysis.*

RANDI HUTTER EPSTEIN, MD, MPH, MS, is writer in residence at the Program for Humanities in Medicine at Yale School of Medicine, a lecturer in the English Department at Yale College, and an adjunct professor of journalism at Columbia University Graduate School of Journalism. She is the author of *Get Me Out* and *Aroused*. She lives in New York City with her husband and is currently quarantining with three of her four grown children.

MIRANDA FEATHERSTONE is a writer and social worker whose fiction has appeared in *Saint Ann's Review*. She lives with her family in Philadelphia.

OCTÁVIO LUIZ MOTTA FERRAZ is a Brazilian legal academic at King's College London, co-director of the Transnational Law Institute, and author of *Health as a Human Right: The Politics and Judicialization of Health in Brazil*.

MONICA FERRELL is the author of three books of poetry and fiction, most recently *You Darling Thing*, a finalist for the Kingsley Tufts Award and *Believer* Book Award in Poetry.

NELL FREUDENBERGER is the author of the novels *Lost and Wanted*, *The Dissident*, and *The Newlyweds*, and the story collection *Lucky Girls*.

ELISA GABBERT is the author of five collections of poetry, essays, and criticism, most recently *The Unreality of Memory & Other Essays* and *The Word Pretty*.

HAFIZAH GETER, born in Zaria, Nigeria, is a writer and editor. She is the author of the poetry collection *Un-American*. Her poetry and prose have appeared in *The New Yorker*, *Boston Review*, *Los Angeles Review of Books*, *Longreads*, and *GAY Magazine*, among others. She lives in Brooklyn.

EMILY GOGOLAK is a writer and reporter from Arizona. She lives in Texas and is a grantee at the Pulitzer Center.

EMILY GREENWOOD is professor of classics at Yale University and holds a secondary appointment in African American studies. She has published books on Thucydides' *History* and the reception of Greek and Roman classics in the modern world.

EMILY ZIFF GRIFFIN is the author of *Light Years,* a novel for young adults inspired by her father's death from AIDS.

BRIALLEN HOPPER is the author of *Hard to Love: Essays and Confessions,* and the co-editor of the online magazine *Killing the Buddha.* Her writing has appeared in *The Los Angeles Review of Books, New York Magazine/The Cut, The Paris Review Daily,* the *Seattle Star,* the *Washington Post,* and elsewhere. She teaches creative nonfiction at Queens College, City University of New York, and lives in Elmhurst, Queens.

MAJOR JACKSON is the author of five books of poetry, most recently *The Absurd Man.* His edited volumes include *Best American Poetry 2019, Renga for Obama,* and Library of America's *Countee Cullen: Collected Poems.* A recipient of a Guggenheim Fellowship, he is the Richard A. Dennis Professor of English and University Distinguished Professor at the University of Vermont. He serves as the poetry editor of *The Harvard Review.*

JOAN NAVIYUK KANE is the author of seven collections of poetry and prose, most recently *Another Bright Departure.* She is the 2019–2020 Hilles Bush Fellow at the Radcliffe Institute for Advanced Study at Harvard University and was a 2018 Guggenheim Fellow.

NOREEN KHAWAJA writes about thought and culture and teaches in the Religion and Modernity Program at Yale University. She is the author of *The Religion of Existence: Asceticism in Philosophy from Kierkegaard to Sartre.*

KHAMEER KIDIA is a Zimbabwean physician at Brigham & Women's Hospital in Boston. His writing has appeared in *The New England Journal of Medicine* and *Annals of Internal Medicine.*

KATIE KITAMURA's most recent novel is *A Separation.*

LAURA KOLBE practices medicine and teaches at Weill Cornell Hospital in New York. Her poems, essays, and fiction have appeared in *American Poetry Review, The New York Review of Books, VQR,* and elsewhere.

YUSEF KOMUNYAKAA's forthcoming collection, *Everyday Mojo Songs of Earth: New and Selected Poems 2001–2021,* will be published in 2021. He teaches at New York University.

KATHRYN LOFTON is a professor of religious studies and of American studies at Yale University.

SEAN LYNCH is a recent graduate of Yale University, where he majored in English.

MILLICENT MARCUS is acting chair of the Italian Department and a member of the faculty in Film and Media Studies at Yale University. She is the author of *An Allegory of Form: Literary Self-Consciousness in "The Decameron."*

LAREN MCCLUNG is the author of *Between Here and Monkey Mountain* and editor of *Inheriting the War: Poetry and Prose by Descendants of Vietnam Veterans and Refugees.*

JOYELLE MCSWEENEY is the author of nine genre-crossing books. With Johannes Göransson, she founded the internationalist press Action Books and teaches in the MFA Program at the University of Notre Dame.

RUSSELL MORSE is a writer and public defender based in New York City. As a journalist, he has covered youth uprisings in France, juvenile justice reform in California, issues along the U.S.–Mexico border, and three presidential elections. His work has appeared in *Rolling Stone* magazine, the *San Francisco Chronicle,* and *Salon.* Morse was awarded a Guggenheim Fellowship in criminal justice for his prison reform work in New York State.

MEGHANA MYSORE is an editorial assistant at *The Yale Review* and a 2020 graduate of Yale, where she majored in English with a concentration in writing. In the fall of 2020, she will begin work on an MFA in fiction at Hollins University.

ERIC O'KEEFE-KREBS is a writer from Queens. He is a student at Yale University, where he studies economics and anthropology.

MEGHAN O'ROURKE is the editor of *The Yale Review.* A recipient of a Guggenheim Fellowship, a Radcliffe Fellowship, and other awards, she is the author of the memoir *The Long Goodbye* and three collections of poetry, most recently *Sun in Days.*

ROWAN RICARDO PHILLIPS is the author of *Living Weapon.*

MAYA C. POPA is the author of *American Faith,* recipient of the 2020 North American Book Prize from the Poetry Society of Virginia. She is a teacher, poetry reviews editor at *Publishers Weekly,* and a PhD candidate at Goldsmiths, University of London.

ROGER REEVES's poems and essays have appeared or are forthcoming from *Poetry, The Believer,* and *Boston Review.* He is an associate professor of poetry at the University of Texas at Austin.

BRANDON SHIMODA's recent books include *The Grave on the Wall,* which received the PEN Open Book Award, *The Desert,* and *Evening Oracle,* which received the William Carlos Williams Award from the Poetry Society of America. He lives in Tucson, Arizona.

RACHEL JAMISON WEBSTER is a professor of creative writing at Northwestern University, a 2019–2020 Kaplan Fellow in the Humanities, and the author of four books of poetry.

JOHN FABIAN WITT is the Allen H. Duffy Class of 1960 Professor of Law and Head of Davenport College at Yale University. His most recent books are *To Save the Country: A Lost Treatise on Martial Law* (with Will Smiley) and *American Contagions.*

RENA XU (MD, MBA) has written on health care delivery for *The New Yorker, The Atlantic,* and *The New England Journal of Medicine.* She is currently a fellow in pediatric urology at Boston Children's Hospital and a Blavatnik Fellow in Life Science Entrepreneurship at Harvard.